THE TIME OF YOUR LIFE

THE TIME OF YOUR LIFE

MORE REFLECTIONS AND POEMS FOR THE YOUNG AT HEART

MARIE KANE-DUDLEY

FOREWORD BY SIMON PONSONBY

CWR

Unless otherwise indicated, all Scripture references are from the Holy
Bible: New International Version (NIV), copyright © 1973, 1978, 1984 by the
International Bible Society.
Other versions used:
The Message: Scripture taken from *THE MESSAGE*. Copyright © by Eugene
H. Peterson, 1993, 1994, 1995, 1996, 2000, 2001, 2002. Used by permission
of NavPress Publishing Group. NASB: *New American Standard Bible*, © 1977,
Lockman Corporation. NKJV: *New King James Version*, © 1982, Thomas
Nelson Inc. TLB: *The Living Bible*, © 1971, 1994, Tyndale House Publishers.
NLT: Scripture quotations marked NLT are taken from the *Holy Bible*, New
Living Translation, copyright © 1996, 2004. Used by permission of Tyndale
House Publishers, Inc., Wheaton, Illinois 60189. All rights reserved.
Concept development, editing, design and production by CWR
Printed in China by 1010 Printing
ISBN: 978-1-85345-682-4

This book is dedicated to the memory of
Arthur, the father of my children,
and to the memory of
Paul, my youngest child

And it is given with love to my children,
Miriam, John, Richard and their families

You have done the impossible by keeping me on my toes
and on my knees, and for that I am so grateful.

'When I think of the wisdom and scope of his plan I
fall down on my knees and pray to the Father of all
the great family of God – some of them already in
heaven and some down here on earth – that out of
his glorious, unlimited resources he will give you the
mighty inner strengthening of his Holy Spirit. And
I pray that Christ will be more and more at home in
your hearts, living within you as you trust in him.
May your roots go down deep into the soil of God's
marvellous love; and may you be able to feel and
understand, as all God's children should, how long,
how wide, how deep, and how high his love really is;
and to experience this love for yourselves, though
it is so great that you will never see the end of it
or fully know or understand it. And so at last
you will be filled up with God himself.'

(Ephesians 3:14–19, TLB)

Acknowledgements

Thanks be to God for the gift of Jesus, and for enabling me to write of His goodness.

I am grateful to my cousin, Oonagh Walker, who proofread all my scripts and whose suggestions were always helpful and kindly given. Thank you, Oonagh.

A huge 'Thank you' to Libby Lake who came to my rescue at a late date and typed the whole book in record time. Libby, you are a star!

My thanks also to Suzie Renno who has agreed to be my PA when the book is published. I'm very grateful, Suzie.

A big 'Thank you' to Sue Kenchington who bravely offered to keep me in right standing with the tax man! Your expertise is such a relief to me, Sue!

To CWR I say 'Thank you' for your encouragement, expertise and patience with someone who hasn't moved into the digital age! Lynette and Sue, you are always so understanding and kind. Thank you too, Carol, for your editing. All your suggestions have been wise and encouraging. Finally, thank you, Simon, for your excellent cover design, and Charlotte, for your detailed work on the internals. I'm very grateful.

My amazed thanks go to Simon Ponsonby who offered to write the foreword to this book. Such a kindness!

I am very grateful to Mark Stibbe for his endorsement of The Time of Your Life; *thank you, Mark.*

Thank you to all the friends who have encouraged me in my writing, and who have prayed for me.

And last, but by no means least, thanks to my children, Miriam and Stuart, John and Jane, Richard and Maria, together with their children, who all helped to launch As Time Goes By *and are now waiting in the wings for the launch of* The Time of Your Life. *You're a wonderful blessing to me. Thank you.*

Contents

Foreword

As I sit down to write this foreword, I have just watched online part of a long sermon recommended to me by a friend. The sermon was given by a dynamic young preacher who has founded a thriving church, filled with young people. He spoke with zeal and passion, wit and cultural connectivity, and insight into his biblical theme. His hair had a little too much gel and stood a little too tall for my liking, but he was very good. I could see why he is very successful, and I was grateful to God that the gospel is being entrusted to faithful young men. But as I listened I couldn't help but think, in the way only a less popular, middle-aged preacher with an expanding waistline can, that he took eighteen minutes to say something worth saying. At least he then had a point, and a good one. Many speakers and many writers take a long time getting nowhere. Not so Marie Kane-Dudley. She has a way of painting something profound, of stirring the emotions and the affections, with just a handful of well-placed words.

I first met Marie at a conference, and what struck me was her depth of spirituality, desire for more of God and a twinkle in her eye. I am delighted to have been asked to commend her latest offering of meditations and poems. It's very easy to do so. For Marie is a woman who has walked with the Lord, who has heard His voice, who has understood His ways, who has been through the fire with Him, who has known life's disappointments and delights, and who has been transformed and conformed into the likeness of the Lord she loves. Marie writes as one with authority – an authority conferred through a life lived and a Saviour known; an authority marinated in grace. In this book, wisdom hard won is distilled in brief, though never trite, memorable meditations. Here is bandage for the bruised, food for the journey, lovers' whispers.

St Paul once wrote of Timothy: 'I am reminded of your sincere faith, a faith that dwelt first in your grandmother Lois …' (2 Tim. 1:5, ESV). As I have read Marie's work, I have often called to mind this verse, and felt that here was sincere faith, being passed on by a 'grand' mother in the faith. I have loved Marie's pastoral and prophetic reflections – and they have helped me.

I hope and pray that many will find this book – and if I ever meet that dynamic young preacher with the tall hair I'll give him a copy.

Rev Simon Ponsonby
Pastor of Theology,
St Aldates Church, Oxford

Introduction

When I was six I had an idol. Miss Hardy was pretty and wore beautiful clothes; she was my teacher. One day, I heard these words fall from her lovely lips, as she spoke to my mother: 'Marie is a plodder.' I squirmed inside because, for some strange reason, I didn't like the sound of that. Many decades later, I have to admit that she was right. My children tell me that for years I talked about writing a book, yet I was approaching eighty before I actually embarked upon the journey. But, like the tortoise, I eventually got there!

The book that emerged, *As Time Goes By*, seems to have been a great blessing to very many people, and this is a surprising joy to me. I am deeply grateful to God that He has given me length of days and the gifting to write a book which tells of His goodness and faithfulness. Encouraged by its success, I continued to write and so was born *The Time of Your Life*.

The Time of Your Life conjures up a picture of life at its very best, when hopes and dreams are being fulfilled and we may even feel delirious with happiness. At such a time we could be tempted to think that heaven has come down to earth and we want nothing more, losing our sense of the BIG picture which is that this blissful time *will* come to an end, for this life is but a preparation for the time of *true* bliss which God has prepared for those who love Him. I believe that God says to each of us, 'This *is* the time of *your* life. It is a gift from Me to you. Use it well.' Time is precious. This life is not a dress-rehearsal; this performance of our lives is the real thing. Each day the play moves on.

And so, in this great Drama of Life there are times and seasons. As we reflect upon our lives we can visualise the seasons as the acts and scenes in our own personal drama, and whatever our time of life we can know that God is with us on stage, waiting to bless us as we allow Him to direct us.

My book is an attempt to help us all to cultivate a heavenly perspective amidst the circumstances of our lives, be they exciting, hard or humdrum. Jesus promised that one day He will return to claim His own. *We* could be in that generation. If not, we will meet Him when we die. Whichever way, our assurance is that one day we will see Him face to face, our Divine Director and Lover who will lead us into the Grand Finale of 'The Divine Romance'.

I hope that the short prayer at the end of each piece will be but a starting point for our own conversations with God who is always waiting to hear from us.

1. *Under the bonnet*

When I married Arthur in 1957, he was the proud
possessor of a car: few people in our circle could make
such a boast.

He told me that, on buying his first car, he drove it home
and immediately dismantled the engine in order to see how it
worked. His next task was to reassemble it, and ever after he did
his own car repairs. Little did I realise how this would affect my
life! Over the years, he spent many hours *under* the car of the
moment and I can clearly picture him in oily overalls, oily rag
in hand and face streaked with oil, coming into the house to
report to me his progress – or lack of it!

Thinking about those days, I realise that Arthur's ears
were finely tuned to the sounds from the engine. I hadn't the
remotest interest in, or idea of, what went on under the bonnet
but sometimes, as we drove along, Arthur would say, 'Can you
hear that pinking? I'll have to look at the tappets.' My heart
would sink as I envisaged him spending yet more hours lying
under the car repairing it. Eventually I too could recognise
the 'pinking' – which I learnt meant 'knocking' – and the
dictionary tells me that a 'tappet' is a mechanical part that
'reciprocates to receive or transmit intermittent motion' – a
mystery to me but maybe not to you! By listening, Arthur could
detect when something was wrong under the bonnet.

I've come to believe that, if we're tuned in, the Holy Spirit can teach us to listen to what's going on under the 'bonnet' of our own hearts. For instance, I realised recently that I do a lot of internal grumbling. Others can't hear it but God can. It's my spiritual 'pinking' and it disturbs my heart, my peace and my ability to continue on my journey with God. As I think about my silent grumbles, I see how petty they are – the queue at the checkout, just missing a bus, difficulty in opening a biscuit packet and so on – little things which I allow to transmit dissatisfaction into the whole of me. I am grateful to the Holy Spirit that He has convicted me of this and reminded me of Proverbs 4:23: 'Above all else, guard your heart, for it is the wellspring of life.'

Once we have been convicted of the sin that disturbs our peace, we have a responsibility to deal with it just as Arthur had to deal with those tappets! In other words, we need to repent, receive God's forgiveness and move on. As we practise living in that way, we will become more sensitive to those spiritual 'pinkings' and the oil of God's Spirit will soothe our inner unease or even dis-ease. '... if we confess our sins to him, he can be depended upon to forgive us and to cleanse us from every wrong' (1 John 1:9, TLB).

We can be totally sure that the oil of the Holy Spirit under the bonnet of our hearts will produce His love, joy and peace in our lives. Each one of us can say with humble confidence, 'I am a work in progress,' and can join with the apostle Paul in saying, 'Not that I have already ... been made perfect, but I press on to take hold of that for which Christ Jesus took hold of me' (Philippians 3:12).

Dear Jesus, I know that I sadden You when I grumble inwardly about the circumstances of the moment. Please help me to obey Your Word and be led by Your Spirit. I know that, when I do so, You give me peace of heart. Thank You, Jesus.

2. *The surrender*

Surrendering goes against the grain. How we like to have our own way! It doesn't surprise us when children squabble over a favourite toy, but do we recognise that same tendency in ourselves? For instance, do we ever, as adults, withdraw into a sulk when we can't watch our preferred TV programme?

Hopefully, as we mature in age and in grace, we become more willing to surrender. We have, of course, the perfect example in Jesus Christ – the totally surrendered Man. It is impossible for us to imagine what He relinquished when, out of love for us, He willingly left the glory and bliss of His heavenly home and submitted Himself to all that is involved in being human. From birth to death and everything in between – the growing, learning and working; the hunger, thirst, fatigue and pain; the betrayed friendships, rejection, loneliness and cruelty – all were experienced by the Surrendered Lamb who was slain so that we might live.

As we contemplate these truths, our hearts are touched and we want to be like Him. In the warmth of the moment we may sing, 'All to Jesus I surrender', and really mean it. But what happens when we face *the big issue*? Many years ago, when I was a new Christian, a priest said that practising a lifestyle of saying 'Yes' to God over small things would ensure that when *the big issue* came along it would be simply natural to say 'Yes' to that. I have to admit that I didn't find it so, but I am comforted when I remember that Jesus Himself struggled in Gethsemane, before going to the cross, praying, 'My Father! If it is possible, let this cup be taken away from me. But I want your will, not mine' (Matthew 26:39, TLB).

Paul was the youngest of our four children. He was a beautiful and gentle child but, as he grew up, we realised that all was not right. His life became chaotic, and in those days we couldn't get the help we sensed he needed. He was an adult before dyslexia and bipolar were diagnosed but sadly, by then, great harm had been done. Because of his problems, I seemed to carry him in my heart for years, praying for him.

One day, during my prayers, the thought of Abraham being asked by God to put Isaac onto the altar came to me. It filled me with fear and dread but, after a struggle, I prayed a prayer which I felt was pulled from the very innermost depths of my being as I gave Paul to God, saying, 'Whatever it takes, Lord'. It was the hardest prayer I'd ever prayed. I then sensed that God asked me to put myself on the altar too and so I did.

Time went by – precious time that God gave us, when Paul and I grew ever closer and were more and more able to express our love for each other. It was obvious that he was very unwell physically but, because of his mental illness, he didn't avail himself of the help he needed. He came to see me almost every day and I did what I could to help him but he needed more than I could give.

In desperation, three days before Christmas Day 2007, I knelt down and cried out to Jesus, 'Please lift Paul out of the mire.' I felt that God said, 'Your prayers have been answered,' and I had an impression of Jesus laying His hands on me and anointing me. I shared this with my friend, Pat, who was Paul's godmother, and also with my prayer partner, Renée, asking them to pray. Pat's response to me was, 'It's time to be praising God.'

On Christmas Eve, Paul was admitted to hospital suffering from pneumonia. As a family, we were all relieved to know that he was receiving proper care at last. But on Christmas morning we were summoned to the hospital. John, my son, got me there as quickly as possible but we were too late. Paul had suffered a cardiac arrest and had died.

This was not the way in which I had envisaged God answering my prayers. The blow was enormous: the shock was huge. And yet those words, 'Your prayers have been answered', were so alive in my spirit. I was further blessed when Jane, my daughter-in-law, told me of a picture she'd had as we prayed before going to the hospital. She 'saw' the hospital room. Angels stood around the walls with bowed heads and Paul was being held by his heavenly Father in a moment of intimacy and sacredness, hence the bowed heads of the angels. And yet another blessing came the next morning when Jane drew my attention to a verse in the day's Bible reading: '... blessed *is* she who believed that there would be a fulfillment of what had been spoken to her by the Lord' (Luke 1:45, NASB). Again, I knew in my spirit that God wanted me to receive that promise.

What have I learnt from that hard experience? Quite simply, to trust God to answer our prayers in the best possible way. As He says in Isaiah 55:8–9, 'For my thoughts are not your thoughts, neither are your ways my ways ... As the heavens are higher than the earth, so are my ways higher than your ways and my thoughts than your thoughts.'

And I believe it touches His Father-heart when one of His children says, 'Even though I don't understand, I will trust You.'

Dear Lord and Father, thank You for the gift of children. Help us to remember that they are first and foremost Yours. Thank You that when I am in pain it is then that You speak most clearly and most dearly to me, if I will only listen.

The wine press

The closer I am to Jesus
The sweeter I shall grow.
But can I submit to the pressing that follows,
So that the wine will flow?

The pressing is so painful;
There's agony in my heart.
Gethsemane brings suffering
And I am torn apart.

Jesus Himself has been there;
His own will He resigned;
For His Father is the Gardener
And Jesus is the Vine.

And I, a grape upon that Vine
Must through the process go;
If I surrender to my Lord
That pressing I shall know.

My life will be like poured-out wine
As I yield to Him my all;
For they must be like Christ Himself
Who answer to this call.

3. *Who do you think you are?*

Perhaps the popular TV programme has prompted you to wonder who *you* are? If we set out to trace our own family tree, we need to be prepared for surprises, some good, some bad. And such an exercise will probably cause us to assess what we've been dealt in life – a good hand or a bad hand – for we all come into the world totally dependent on the family into which we are born, with all its particular ways. So, in that sense, each person's inheritance is unique.

However, when we look beyond, we discover that in fact we all have a common ancestor, Adam, and from him we share a common heritage, which is the tendency to sin. 'Surely I was sinful at birth, sinful from the time my mother conceived me' (Psalm 51:5). Apart from Jesus every single person was born into this world a sinner. We are born with a sinful nature which urges us to centre our lives on 'self', rather than upon God. Sin divides us from God and therefore, spiritually, we are all born in helpless poverty.

The good news is that God made a way to lift us out of that poverty and to shower us with riches. To do that, it cost God dearly, for Jesus left His heavenly home and came to earth in order to become the 'second Adam'. When we put our faith in Jesus and in what He did for us on the cross, we are born again by the Holy Spirit and God adopts us into His family. That offer is for everyone.

I've been privileged to witness, within my own family, the wonderful position of adopted children. My brother, Andrew, and his wife, Tricia, adopted four children as babies. There was no doubt at all that each of those children was treated as their very own. Parental love was showered upon them. Everything their parents had was theirs. They *knew* that they belonged and never doubted their identity as children of Andrew and Tricia. Of course, many adopted children do have a deep need to discover their birth parents, but the truth remains that, whatever the circumstances of a baby's birth, we all have a heavenly Father waiting to adopt us.

So ... do *we* know who we are? If we have accepted God's gift of Jesus, Father has adopted us into His family. We are loved by Him – John 16:27. He calls each of us His child – John 1:12. He has good plans for us – Jeremiah 29:11. Nothing can separate us from His love – Romans 8:39. Those are just a few of our privileges! And if we have any doubts, we should remember the words of Jesus who said, 'When you pray, say "Father".' He used the Aramaic word *Abba* – an intimate term for father, used by both children and adults, much as a child today would say 'Daddy'.

And finally, one of my favourite verses, spoken by Jesus to Mary Magdalene after His resurrection, 'I am returning to my Father and your Father, to my God and your God' (John 20:17).

Father, please help me to remember who I am in Christ. May I live as Your child under Your blessings, so delighting Your Father-heart.

4. *Trust*

The human heart seems to have an innate desire to trust and to be trusted. How awesome it is to realise that God, our Creator, longs for us to trust *Him*! More awesome still, to realise that He entrusts us, His creatures, with the gift of free will, which gives us the freedom to choose to trust or not to trust Him.

Scripture advises us: 'Trust in the LORD with all your heart, and lean not on your own understanding; in all your ways acknowledge Him, and He shall direct your paths' (Proverbs 3:5–6, NKJV).

In his book, *My Utmost for His Highest*, Oswald Chambers says, 'We enthrone common sense and tack the name of God on the end. We *do* lean on our own understanding instead of trusting God with all our hearts' (my emphasis). Indeed, how hard we find it to trust God when the circumstances are bleak!

We can learn a lot about the nature of trust by observing little children. Did not Jesus Himself say, 'unless you ... become like little children, you will never enter the kingdom of heaven' (Matthew 18:3)? Simple, childlike trust is what God desires from us. My own heart is touched when a small child puts his little hand into mine in complete trust. I know that, if danger were to rear its head, that child would cling to me all the closer, trusting me to be his protector.

When my grandson, Sam, was a toddler, I often had the role of babysitter. Sam's security had been deeply disturbed by the death of his beloved 'Grandpa' – my husband, Arthur. I recall that, as I tucked him into bed, his final words were always the same: 'Good night and God bless you. See you in the morning. Will you leave the bedroom door open? Will you leave the sitting room door open? And will you ask Mum and Dad to come and see me when they get home?' As he spoke out his little requests and plans, he was reassuring himself – that Mum and Dad *would* be coming home, we *would* all be seeing each other in the morning; and open doors meant easy contact.

As adults, we still have that need of security and therefore, like Sam, we try to ensure our safety in a variety of ways. We may put our trust in a career, in marriage, in owning a home, or in a good insurance plan, a pension scheme, a burglar-proof house or many other things. Advertising urges us to protect ourselves against every possible catastrophe. Yet, of course, we have to admit that all these things are themselves at risk of failing; for sadly, many marriages break down, careers are no longer for a lifetime, homes can be repossessed, pension schemes can fail. People are shaken by such facts of life and many, in desperation, turn to drugs or alcohol and, even more tragically, to suicide.

How sad it would be had we to end on that note! But thankfully we can know beyond doubt that God has said He will never leave us nor forsake us (Joshua 1:5; Matthew 28:20). And Psalm 91 declares that God will be with us in trouble and that when we call on Him, He *will* answer us. In my own life, I've found Him to be true to His promises. Life is not easy, but just as a child only really discovers the faithfulness of his parents when he, himself, is in a crisis situation, so we, too – God's children – learn more of His love and presence during the hard times.

Dear heavenly Father, I long to have a childlike trust in You. Holy Spirit, please help me to remember that, whatever is going on in my life, my Father's outstretched hand is waiting to feel my hand in His. Thank You, Lord, for Your faithfulness.

5. *The pink umbrella*

I needed a new umbrella. Wouldn't you think that by the time I'd reached the age of eighty I'd have some common sense? Well, if I had, it flew out of the window the moment I saw the pink umbrella. In my heart, I knew that a collapsible one, which would fold away into a neat little package, was the sensible option; but oh, how the pink one appealed! It was a long, non-collapsible umbrella with a candy pink curved handle. When opened, its cup-shaped dome was of clear plastic with a pink trim. I bought it!

To be truthful, it really was a cumbersome thing to take shopping and, deep down, I knew that a collapsible one would have been so much more suited to my needs. But I did like it! All I needed were lots of rainy days when the only thing I had to carry was my pink umbrella – with me underneath its clear plastic dome, I was sure that we made a pretty sight! But, whenever rain was forecast, I could be seen struggling with my shopping bags and the beautiful but awkward umbrella. I didn't like to admit to myself that the pink umbrella was a beautiful but big mistake. I knew that the Queen had a similar one but, of course, she didn't have to cope with shopping bags!

Then came a day of shopping in a nearby town. Complete with bags and pink umbrella, I did all that had to be done and then boarded the bus for the half-hour journey home. Reality hit me when we were midway between Romsey and Winchester: I had my shopping bags but I did not have my pink umbrella! My heart plummeted. I felt the loss as I tried to relive my movements, hoping that somehow I'd be able to retrieve it. But my imagination led me to picturing someone seizing the umbrella with glee and making it their own. My heart felt hurt that anyone could be so *mean*. But how mean were my condemnatory thoughts, for in my imaginings I gave no credence to the possibility that the finder might have done the honourable thing and handed in my umbrella to the appropriate person. The hurt and criticism took control, and misery overwhelmed me until eventually I came to my senses. 'This is all wrong,' I breathed, 'Please help me, Lord.' And, of course, He did. A thought came to me: I could pray that whoever had found it would be blessed and would enjoy my pink umbrella. What a happy release!

God then blessed me again, for I began to admit that it had been a ridiculously impractical umbrella for me. Was He laughing at me – ever so gently? A sense of relief swept over me. I was no longer encumbered with it; I was free to go and buy a collapsible one. I might even find a pink one! God's patience with my aged foolishness constantly amazes me. Nevertheless, I am sure that He wants me to apply the lessons I've learnt from my pink umbrella to other 'things' in my life.

Dear Lord, I'm sorry that I allow 'things' to become too important to me. When I do, I know that they become idols, replacing You. Please forgive me and help me to keep You at the centre of my life.

My Teacher

Jesus, Your Godhead surrendered,
Vulnerability accepted,
Totally.

Helpless, dependent,
Willing to be taught,
Completely.

Your life is my lesson.

Help me to surrender the desire
To be in control of my life.
Help me to trust You
With a childlike trust,
To be an eager pupil
Learning from You, my Master,
Jesus.

6. *A traveller's tale*

After seventeen years of life in the South of England, I confess that a northern accent is music to my ears. When I hear one, I usually enter into conversation with this other 'foreigner'. Northerners are such friendly folk!

One such encounter developed into something rather remarkable. I was in a small tearoom in Romsey, filling in time whilst waiting for the bus to Winchester. A man came in and sat at the table next to mine. When he gave his order I recognised a northern accent and we were soon in conversation. I learnt that he came from Liverpool – the wrong side of the Pennines perhaps but, nevertheless, a Northerner – and so our chat continued.

After a while, he asked what had taken me into Romsey so I explained that I'd been to the Christian bookshop in connection with the promotion of my recently published book, *As Time Goes By*. Not surprisingly, he then asked what the book was about. I told him that it consisted mainly of stories from my own life – stories which demonstrate how God has helped me in every circumstance, but especially in the hard times, which include the deaths of two husbands and my youngest son.

His face softened as he listened with profound interest. He then told me that he had himself been living through a very hard ten years but was feeling that he could begin to see the light at the end of an extremely dark tunnel. I sensed that his spirit was open, and I felt able to talk to him about the life, death and resurrection of Jesus Christ and the hope this brings to all who believe. I sensed that he had heard the gospel in the past and, like me, he was sure that God had arranged our meeting. He was happy for me to pray for him in that tearoom. Before we parted, I told him of the forthcoming visit to Winchester Cathedral of the evangelist, J. John. Although he'd told me that he travelled a lot, I gave him my phone number in case he had the opportunity to get to a meeting and needed details.

The following day I received a phone call from him. He had found the Christian bookshop and had purchased two of my books – one for his mother and one for his lady friend. He said they both loved it. He then told me that he was with the band, 'Simply Red'. I'd never heard of the band but I now know that everyone else has! Finally, he asked me to pray for him.

In his wonderful book, *My Utmost for His Highest*, Oswald Chambers says, 'God engineers our circumstances.' God is with us in every situation, the good and the bad, and He speaks to us in the midst of them. Our part is to say, 'Speak, Lord, Your servant is listening', and then to obey Him. It is then that we receive His peace.

Heavenly Father, You watch over me and all my activities with tender care. Thank You for the people You bring into my life. Please change my heart to make it more like Yours and help me to treat them as You would want me to.

7. Rejection

A childhood episode which remains clear in my memory relates to an invitation to a birthday party. Now, in the very poor, working-class community in which I grew up, invitations to parties were virtually unknown, so this was a remarkable event.

Birthdays were certainly celebrated in my own home, but just within the immediate family. You'll understand why when I tell you that by the age of eight I had five younger siblings. Nevertheless, our parents made each of us feel very special on our birthday. A card on the doormat in the morning, a small present on the breakfast table, and a delicious tea with a cake and candles (which had to be blown out with one big breath while everyone sang 'Happy birthday to you'), all combined to ensure that we did indeed have 'happy birthdays'. But, as I said, they were essentially family occasions.

I therefore felt very important when, one day, a girl called Clara from the class above me invited me to her birthday party the following Sunday. My family too was duly impressed and, when the big day came, I sallied forth, quietly excited, and dressed in my best frilly frock. Arriving at the house, I knocked on the door, which was opened by a woman who looked at me blankly. 'I've come for the party,' I said, rather tentatively. 'There's no party here,' was her brusque response, as the door was shut in my face. Had I misunderstood? Was it a cruel hoax? Or had Clara, in issuing her invitations, been indulging in a sad little fantasy of what she would like to happen? Who knows? But how foolish and rejected I felt as I made my way home!

A much more disturbing story than mine concerns a young man whom my husband and I were trying to help, many years ago. We recognised that he was suffering from rejection, and this was confirmed when we heard his story. When he was ten years old, he and his two brothers were taken by their father to the local park, where he gave each of them 50p, said 'Goodbye', and walked out of their lives forever. I felt a great sense of shock at such heartlessness. He then told us that, as a baby, his father's father had been found abandoned on a church doorstep. He did not say whether his own father had been deserted, but it seemed that a pattern of hurtful rejection had brought about a hardening of hearts – perhaps as a way to escape more hurt – and that this tragedy was being repeated down through the generations.

Of course, it is impossible to go through life without, at some point, suffering rejection. As children, it hurts, for instance, if we aren't selected for the school team, especially if we believe we deserve to be! And, as we grow older, we encounter many circumstances in modern life which cause humiliation and pain. Redundancy and unemployment cause deep wounds for many people. The deserted partner of a broken marriage suffers a huge sense of rejection. Others may be unable to meet the expectations or demands put upon them and so feel the isolation and despair of failure. But hardening of the heart in the hope of avoiding further pain only causes more unhappiness.

Thankfully, it is possible for every child of God to allow those hurts to be healed and for them to recover. The wonderful truth is that Almighty God is also our Father who loves each of us personally and will *never* reject us. We can feed on God's Word and it is balm to our troubled souls. Jesus Himself said, '... the Father himself loves you dearly because you love me and believe that I came from the Father' (John 16:27, TLB). And from the Old Testament, 'Can a mother forget her little child and not have love for her own son? Yet even if that should be, I will not forget you' (Isaiah 49:15, TLB). How wise we are if we put our faith in verses such as these, for they are medicine to our troubled souls.

The other great blessing we have is this: good churches have pastoral teams who are there to continue the ministry of Jesus. Remember, He came to heal the broken-hearted and to set the captive free and He has followers today who are available to help anyone who is in need.

I have found that, even in the most difficult of circumstances, it is possible to have that deep joy which the world cannot understand. Indeed, to know that we are loved by God is the most joyful of 'knowings'.

Dear Lord, please help me to believe that You will never reject me; that You are waiting with open arms to embrace me. Help me to receive Your love.

The Touch of the Master's Hand

'Twas battered and scarred, and the auctioneer
Thought it scarcely worth his while
To waste much time on the old violin,
But held it up with a smile.
'What am I bidden, good folks,' he cried,
'Who'll start bidding for me?'
'A dollar, a dollar'; then 'Two! Only two?
Two dollars, who'll make it three?
Three dollars, once; three dollars, twice;
Going for three –' But no,
From the room, far back, a gray-haired man
Came forward and picked up the bow;
Then, wiping the dust from the old violin,
And tightening the loose strings,
He played a melody pure and sweet
As a caroling angel sings.

The music ceased, and the auctioneer,
With a voice that was quiet and low,
Said: 'What am I bid for the old violin?'
And he held it up with the bow.
'A thousand dollars, and who'll make it two?
Two thousand! And who'll make it three?
Three thousand, once; three thousand, twice;
And going, and gone,' said he.
The people cheered, but some of them cried,

'We do not quite understand
What changed its worth?' Swift came the reply:
'The touch of a master's hand.'

And many a man with life out of time,
And battered and scarred with sin,
Is auctioned cheap to the thoughtless crowd,
Much like the old violin.
A 'mess of pottage,' a glass of wine;
A game – and he travels on.
He is 'going' once, and 'going' twice,
He's 'going' and almost 'gone'.
But the Master comes, and the foolish crowd
Never can quite understand,
The worth of a soul and the change that's wrought
By the touch of the Master's hand.

Written by Myra Brooks Welch and first published in
the February 26, 1921, issue of *The Gospel Messenger*
(now called *Messenger*), the denominational magazine
of the Church of the Brethren.

8. *Heart prints*

Wherever I go, I leave them. No, I'm not talking about my gloves, my glasses or my umbrella! I'm talking about something no one can see – my fingerprints. Like it or not, we leave our fingerprints everywhere. That is simply a fact of life.

But another fact of life is this: wherever we go we leave 'heart prints'. By our words and actions we imprint hearts. That is an awesome responsibility. I'm sure we can all look back over our lives and remember the people who did our hearts good. Sadly, too, we will recall those who hurt our hearts. Of course, we know that in our close relationships we are touching the hearts of others, but I believe that in our chance encounters also we can imprint hearts.

I love to picture this story. While William McKinley was campaigning for the presidency of the United States of America at the turn of the twentieth century, a certain young reporter constantly harassed him – a real 'thorn in the flesh'. One bitterly cold night, as William approached his coach, he saw the young man waiting for him. Noticing that the reporter had no coat and was shivering in the icy wind, William stopped, took off his own coat and said to the embarrassed young journalist, 'Here, have my coat and ride inside with me.' Stammering, the young man said, 'But you don't know me. I'm the one who's been giving you such a hard time.' 'Of course I know you,' came the reply, 'but it makes no difference. Put on the coat and come inside where it's warm.'

We can be sure that the young reporter would never forget that heart-printing action.

That story reminds me of one Jesus told. A lone traveller was set upon by robbers who, after stealing his belongings, left him to die. Two religious people walked past him, ignoring his plight. Then, along came a despised Samaritan who stopped, attended to the suffering man's wounds, lifted him onto his own beast and took him to the nearest inn, where he arranged and paid for his care (Luke 10:25–37). Jesus then asked His listeners which of the three men who passed by on the road was a neighbour to the wounded man. 'The one who had mercy on him,' came the reply. 'Go and do likewise,' said Jesus. And, if we listen, we will hear Him say that to us too.

It costs to be merciful. Mother Teresa once said that loneliness was a greater scourge in the West than poverty in the Third World. Perhaps the best heart-printing gift we can leave with someone is our time, if it is given with a listening ear and a compassionate heart. Jesus Himself is the perfect example of a person of generosity and compassion. He *gave up* everything so that we could *have* everything.

Dear Jesus, please help me to open my heart more and more to You. Only then will my heart prints on others be like Yours.

Receiving God's love

You cry out to Me, 'Come, Lord Jesus.'
I cry out to you, 'Come, my child.'
Remember, if you draw near to Me, I will draw near
*   to you. That is My promise to you.*
Heart to heart lovers! When you know Me in that way,
*   you're in the element for which you were created.*
Listen afresh with a new, listening heart: I love you.
Let your heart be touched by those words. Jesus, your
*   Lover, longs for you to love Him.*

Remember, My birth was in a cold, bare, unbeautiful
stable but I came to that place and transformed it.
However cold, bare and unbeautiful your heart is, I long
to come in and transform it. Don't let guilt or shame
hold you back. As you come to Me for forgiveness, I will
respond to your invitation, enter in and transform your
love and your life. Will you trust Me?

9. *Bearing fruit in old age*

Can you remember the days when you were always wishing to be older – old enough to go to bed later; old enough to go to the corner shop on your own; old enough to use a pen?

Later on, the 'wish list' was different. I remember wishing I were old enough to wear make-up, have a perm, go to a dance, have a boyfriend, get married and have children. And, as time went by, all these things happened.

But then came the day when, looking in the mirror, I gasped! Was that really a grey hair – and surely that couldn't be a wrinkle? 'I must be getting old,' I thought, 'and I don't want to!' So I tried not to notice the birthdays too much but, the older I got, the more my family seemed to want to celebrate. I tried to convince myself that, although the years were mounting up, I still felt and looked young. That is, until the awful day when I overheard someone refer to 'that elderly lady'. I looked around to see her. There was no one there! Surely *I* wasn't 'the elderly lady'? But, of course, I was. So, that was it: time to face reality and consider how best to live in *this* season of life.

Spring and autumn are my favourite seasons and I think that those 'of a certain age' are in the season of autumn. In his 'Ode to Autumn', the poet John Keats described it as the 'Season of mists and mellow fruitfulness'. Sadly perhaps, the sight, the hearing and the memory *could* be described as somewhat 'misty' but I like the idea of 'mellow fruitfulness'.

I am reminded of Psalm 92:12,14 in which the psalmist

declares: 'The righteous will ... still bear fruit in old age, they will stay fresh and green ...' I've come to realise that, rather than resist the idea of being elderly, I should be so grateful to God for giving me length of days. For it is He who has numbered my days; therefore, every day is a precious gift from Him (Psalm 139:16).

Jesus said that He had come to give us life, life in abundance. Now, abundance speaks to me of fruitfulness, and I do desire to bear fruit at this stage of my life. Our ageing bodies may limit our activities, but our spirits do not age, and Jesus gave us the secret to a life of fruitfulness: 'I am the vine; you are the branches. If a man remains in me and I in him, he will bear much fruit; apart from me you can do nothing' (John 15:5). How do we remain in Him? By spending time in His presence, which means practising being still, and opening our hearts to His voice and His love; and by reading and obeying His Word. Trying to live according to Jesus' instructions in John 15 is a good starting point. And we can read about the lovely fruit of the Spirit in Galatians: love, joy, peace, patience, kindness, goodness, faithfulness, gentleness and self-control (5:22–23).

So, the autumn of life can be a very beautiful time when God often surprises us with joy, even in the midst of the inevitable difficulties that come as our bodies age. Let's try to remember that every day is a gift and that we are still here in order to fulfil *His* purposes.

Thank You, Lord, for the gift of life and for length of days. Please help me to allow Your Holy Spirit to lead me so that I may bear much fruit for You.

10. *Food on the table*

What a blessing it is to have food on the table! I was brought up in a home where 'grace' was said before and after every meal – recognising that blessing.

Looking back on my childhood, I have good reason to thank both God and my parents that three times a day we sat around the table to eat. We were very poor: for many years, my father worked faithfully, as a bus driver, giving his entire weekly wage of £3 10s (shillings) to my mother, who worked equally hard and sacrificially, to keep all nine of us children fed and watered!

Our diet was basic and, three times a week, my mother baked a big batch of bread; but on Sundays we fed like kings – or so it felt! Because the oven was on for the Sunday roast, my mother also baked cakes and pastry. Quite remarkable! During the week, we went home each day at midday for our dinner, when we'd have a hot but very simple dish followed by a rice pudding. Very occasionally, our amazing mother would surprise us with a steamed pudding and that, for us, was a 'red letter day'. I always hoped that such a treat was awaiting us, and I smile as I recall that we'd often burst into the kitchen asking, not, 'What's for pudding?' but 'What's for rice?' – rice being such a staple of that midday meal that we thought it was the name of the second course!

Many years have passed since those days but I can say, with a thankful heart, that I have always had food on the table. I cannot imagine what it must be like to be hungry and without the means to satisfy that hunger. Starvation must be a terrible way to die.

An important fact for us all to realise is that just as our bodies need to be fed and watered in order to live, so do our spirits. How do we feed our spirits? In Psalm 23 – so well known to us – David declares, 'You provide delicious food for me in the presence of my enemies' (v.5, TLB). So, what has God placed on our table? He has given us His Word and His Holy Spirit as food and drink. Jesus Himself said, 'The Spirit gives life ... The words I have spoken to you are spirit and they are life' (John 6:63) and, again, 'Do not work for food that spoils, but for food that endures to eternal life, which the Son of Man will give you' (John 6:27). We are fed by God's Word and watered by His Spirit.

When my parents put the food on the table we were hungry for it and *we* did the eating and the drinking. Are we hungry enough to dine at God's table every day, and at least twice a day? Are we wise enough to commit verses to memory so that in the bad moments the Holy Spirit can bring them into our minds and we are strengthened? How thankful we should be that God has put food on our tables for both body and spirit.

Lord, please help me to be hungry for You, to desire to feast at Your table. The greatest tragedy would be if I died of starvation because I wouldn't eat.

11. *Dealing with problems – faith or fear?*

I was once told the following story:
A zoo keeper took his friend to observe a strange and interesting happening at the zoo. A snake lay coiled up in the corner of a cage and a small bird was perched on a high beam, as far from the snake as was possible. There the bird sat, gazing at its enemy as though mesmerised. The snake stared unflinchingly at the bird. Then, such a strange thing happened. The tiny bird flew down to the floor and began to hop towards the motionless snake, seemingly unable to avert its eyes from the cold stare of its enemy. Across the floor it hopped until it reached the snake, at which point the crafty reptile opened its mouth and the little bird hopped straight in.

A chilling tale, don't you think? Certainly, the bird had the ability to remain high above the snake but the snake was able to hypnotise the bird, luring it to its death. 'How foolish of the bird,' we think. But sadly, it's all too easy for us to behave like that small bird.

Let me try to explain. Perhaps there are problems in our lives, and I think you'll agree that life is littered with problems. These can be worrying and alarming, such as sickness, money concerns, a difficult marriage or bereavement, to mention but a few. There is no denying that these are hard to bear and are just as real as that snake. The question is: how do we deal with them? For, although we *have* to live through them, we can choose *how* we'll live through them. The negative way is to keep looking at the problem, meditating on it and speculating about it with the great 'What if?' In so doing, we allow FEAR to grip our hearts, which can result in loss of sleep, loss of appetite, depression, illness and even death. This is the road Satan would have us take. Jesus warned us of this, saying, 'The thief comes only to steal and kill and destroy ...' (John 10:10). As the bird hopped into the mouth of the snake and met its end, we can walk into the cavern of fear, making it our dwelling place.

Thankfully, there *is* an alternative way of living. Jesus said, 'I have come that [you] may have life, and have it to the full' (John 10:10). But how do we manage to live abundantly in the midst of hard circumstances? We put FAITH into action! The first thing we must do is to run to God. Talk to Him about the problem, being honest with Him about our feelings. We can ask Him to guide us as to what we can do in the situation and then obey His directions. Sometimes, the answer may be: 'Just pray and wait.' Psalm 23 is a psalm of great solace. The second thing we must consciously do is to put the situation into His hands. We can use our imaginations and actually picture ourselves doing just that. Because we are weak, we may have to do this repeatedly. That's fine with God! We then thank Him that He is taking care of everything in the best possible way and praise Him because He is God and always worthy of praise.

As we practise keeping our eyes on Jesus, with love and trust, He gives us peace of heart, even in the midst of the trials of life.

In this way, we choose life, not death. A scripture I often pray is Proverbs 3:5–6 (NIV, alternative version):

Trust in the LORD with all your heart
and lean not on your own understanding;
in all your ways acknowledge him,
and he will direct your paths.

Lord, You know my foolishness. I so readily walk into the cavern of fear when a problem arises, choosing to let that cavern be my dwelling place, even though You said, 'Do not let your hearts be troubled. Trust in God ...' (John 14:1). I am so sorry for disobeying You. Please forgive me and help me to replace my fear with faith in Your Word.

I'll seek Your dreams

Your patience overwhelms me,
I bow down at Your throne,
And say, 'Please come to be the Lord
Of all I am and own.'

I'm touched by Your compassion;
I wonder at Your love;
My love for You is deepening
As I think on things above.

I lift my eyes to heaven,
Oh, let me hear You speak.
I'll dream the dreams You give me,
For Your face alone I seek.

12. *Jesus and Jim*

I am so comforted by the words Jesus spoke to poor 'doubting Thomas': '... blessed are those who have not seen and yet have believed' (John 20:29). All who put their faith in Jesus are truly blessed.

In his book, *Awake My Heart*, J. Sidlow Baxter tells this beautiful story. Many years ago an Anglican clergyman, in a town in southern England, was looking out of his window at midday and saw a rather rough-looking man going into the church. The same thing happened on several consecutive days; his curiosity was aroused. He therefore asked his verger to keep an eye on the man. This is what he saw: the man entered the church, stuffed his cap into a pocket and walked up to the altar where he stood with bowed head. He then put his hands onto the Communion rail, looked towards the Communion Table and, in a quiet voice, said, 'Jesus, it's Jim,' bowed his head, then quietly left the church.

Some days later, Jim was involved in an accident and was admitted to hospital where he was placed in a ward of the rowdiest, coarsest collection of men the nurses had ever encountered. Indeed, some of the young nurses had been reduced to tears by the men's behaviour. However, after Jim had been there for a few days, there was a marked improvement in the atmosphere of the ward, so much so that the Ward Sister asked one of the men what had brought about this change. 'Oh, it's that chap in the fifth bed. They call 'im Jim,' was the reply. So when the screen was round Jim's bed, the Sister said, 'Jim, you've made such a difference in this ward. How have you done it?' Very simply, Jim replied, 'Well, Sister, I don't know whether you'll understand, but every day, just about 12.30, I see Jesus coming towards the end o' my bed. He stands there for a minute, then He just puts His hand on the bed rail, an' leans over an' says, 'Jim, it's Jesus.'*

As I think about Jim, I'm reminded once again of those other words of Jesus: '... unless you ... become like little children, you will never enter the kingdom of heaven' (Matthew 18:3). Jim *simply believed*. Oh, for that childlike faith and trust!

Dear Jesus, please forgive my doubts and fears. Dear Holy Spirit, please help me to 'simply believe' and to trust God with all my heart. Thank You.

13. *Faith*

On Monday 26 June 2000 a 38-year-old British man named Adrian Nicholas fulfilled his greatest ambition which was to prove that a parachute designed in 1485 by Leonardo da Vinci would work. Using only tools and materials that would have been available 500 years ago, a parachute was constructed. Using it, Adrian Nicholas made a jump from two miles above the Mpumalanga province of South Africa, gliding down 7,000 feet before cutting himself free and landing safely. Leonardo's parachute also floated down safely to the ground. Half a millennium after his death, Leonardo da Vinci was proved right by a man who believed in him and dared to put his faith into action. A newspaper heading read, 'A Leap of Faith'.

I'm reminded of the time when I broke my wrist. Six weeks later, when the plaster was removed, my physiotherapist friend looked at my arm and said, 'You've lost some there.' I saw what she meant – the muscle wastage was quite a shock, and unknown to me it was what had been going on under the plaster due to lack of use of the muscles. And so it is with faith; if we don't use it, we lose it.

I think it's possible to say, 'I believe in God', but if my actions belie my words, my faith will surely weaken. The apostle James tells us: '... faith by itself, if it is not accompanied by action, is dead' (James 2:17).

Faith is at the heart of life, for the truth is that we are all constantly exercising faith – but in what are we putting our faith? Consider for a moment the following situations. We feel ill, so we trust the doctor to prescribe the medicine and the pharmacist to dispense it. We then obey the directions believing we'll recover. Faith!

We put the car key into the ignition and turn it, believing that the engine will spring into life. We then pull into the road, trusting in the road signs and believing that all other road users will obey the Highway Code. We apply the brake, never doubting that the car will stop. Faith!

And when we board a plane, a ferry, a train or a bus, we are trusting so many people and putting our faith in them – from the inventor, the makers and the maintenance crews right through to the pilot or driver. Faith!

Yes, we are always exercising faith in people, things and systems. This rather frightening realisation could cause us to withdraw from a normal, active life for fear of being let down. How foolish that would be!

But perhaps that is how we act with God. He asks us to believe in Him and to trust Him, even showing His love for us by sending His only begotten Son, Jesus, to die for us so that all who believe in Him have assurance of heaven. 'For God so loved the world that he gave his one and only Son, that whoever believes in him shall not perish but have eternal life' (John 3:16). If we act upon God's promises our faith muscle becomes stronger and, more importantly, we are pleasing God, for 'without faith it is impossible to please God' (Hebrews 11:6). There is no greater joy for human parents than to know that their children trust and believe in them. How much more so for our heavenly Father when we put our faith in Him and act it out in love?

Lord, I long to please You. Please give me the grace to choose to put my faith in You and then to act it out in my life. I choose to live by faith.

The King will surely come

The day will come, that awesome day
When the King will surely come
In glory, on the clouds of heaven
In majesty, the King will come.

As lightning flashes in the sky,
Rending the dark of night,
From East to West all eyes shall see
His glory and His might.

And, surely, every ear shall hear
The angels' trumpet call,
When all whom He has called His own
Are lifted to His throne.

Yes, surely, the King will come,
Yet He, Himself, did say,
'Will any faith be found on earth
When I return that day?'

We know not when that day will be
But Wisdom says, 'Prepare,
Choose now, today, to bow the knee
And give your heart in prayer.'

Maranatha – Come, Lord Jesus.

14. *What's in a day?*

My friend, Jean, has the following message on her answer phone: 'This is the day that the Lord has made; let us rejoice and be glad in it.' Unique and challenging, don't you think?

What's in a day? Time-wise, there are twenty-four hours or 1,440 minutes. Now let's imagine that a generous benefactor offered to deposit £1,440 into your account every morning with the proviso that every pound be used well, before the end of the day, and any money not used would be withdrawn. I'm sure that not a single pound would be wasted. Should we not be equally careful with the use of the time God gives us?

Time is elusive. We can't get hold of it; we can't save some today to use another day; and when it's gone it can't be retrieved. We talk about 'spending time', and certainly the day will come for each of us when we make our last withdrawal on 'The Bank of Time'. We will then meet Jesus, who will ask us to give an account of *how* we spent our time.

A lady of ninety-seven wrote out the following short memo for me:

> *Yesterday is history,*
> *Tomorrow is a mystery,*
> *Today is a gift:*
> *That is why we call it 'the present'.*

Perhaps we take 'the present' for granted, until life is threatened and we realise how precious it is. Psalm 1 tells us how to live as God would have us live: delighting in obeying Him and avoiding those who scoff at Him. We learn to live in that way by 'spending time' meditating on God and His Word. I'm well aware of how far I fall short of God's vision for me, but every day is 'a present' – another opportunity to grow a little more in grace.

For many people today, there's never enough time to do all that's demanded of them. Pressures can be colossal. Stress is an epidemic and some may even feel 'enslaved' to their jobs, working all hours and at weekends. I feel very sorry for all who are caught in such a trap. It is not God's way for them.

At the other end of the spectrum, I see that we live in an age when entertainment is available at the mere touch of a button. So many people spend a great part of every day 'being entertained', mainly by the screen which dominates most sitting rooms – the TV – or other electronic and computer games. And sadly, in the world of entertainment in our culture, mocking God is often considered to be clever. Our consciences can become dulled when repeatedly subjected to words and images which are offensive to God and, therefore, should be offensive to us. Perhaps a good slogan could be: 'When in doubt, switch off.'

It's good for us to have leisure time and pursuits, but achieving a balanced lifestyle is a challenge. Jesus Himself enjoyed a party and a picnic, but He also spent much time in prayer, listening to and receiving instructions from His heavenly Father. That's why Jesus always 'got it right'; living as God directed Him. We can be sure that He had the right balance in His daily life.

Surely we should let Him be our role model. Withdrawing from the busy world and resting in His Presence is necessary for a balanced life. In a musical performance the 'rests' are as necessary as the notes played and it's often in the quiet that the music can speak most powerfully. So it is with the performance of our lives. The 'rest' is when God can speak into our souls. What a privilege! What a good use of time! And we find that as we trust and obey Him, He gives us His peace.

Thank You, Lord, for the 'present' of today. Please help me to value the 'now' and to use my time well. I pray that when I meet You face to face I will hear those wonderful words, 'Well done, good and faithful servant ... Enter into the joy of your lord' (Matthew 25:21, NKJV).

Time after time

Time after time the sun has arisen,
Time after time I've seen the moon shine,
Time after time spring's followed winter;
Signs of new life – to my spirit, like wine.

Who is behind such a mighty creation?
Who keeps His hand on the time and the tide?
Surely it is the God of all history,
Whose love is so deep, so high and so wide.

But time after time I offend this dear Father,
Time after time I wound His great heart,
Yet time after time He accepts my repentance
And time after time I receive a fresh start.

So Father, I ask as I bow down before You
For grace to delight You, time after time;
Help me to hear Your voice ever guiding
And then to obey You, time after time.

15. *Saving the starfish*

I'm sure you feel as I do when you're made aware of so much suffering, so much need, and so much pain in the world. It's all too awful; we want to help, but our offering seems too small to make a difference.

In his book, *The Star Thrower*, Loren Eiseley tells this story. One day he was walking along a beach where thousands of starfish had been washed up. He was intrigued by the sight of a boy picking them up one by one and throwing them back into the ocean. He stopped to speak. 'Why are you doing this?' he asked. 'If I don't, they'll die,' said the boy. 'But how can saving such a few make a difference when so many are doomed?' asked the author. The young boy picked up another starfish, threw it into the ocean and said, 'It's going to make a lot of difference to *this* one.'

Eiseley went home to continue writing but he couldn't type a single word. Instead, he returned to the beach and spent the rest of the day helping the boy to throw starfish back into the ocean!*

Surely there's a lesson for us in that story. In our world there is an ocean of suffering and lack, and many people must feel they've been beached on a hard shore. With childlike simplicity, the young boy did what he could, undaunted by the hugeness of the problem. The little bit he did made a life-changing difference to some of the starfish. In just the same way, our acts of kindness to people, whether personally or through charities, *will* make a difference. Give as giving unto the Lord, for He Himself said, '... whatever you did for one of the least of these brothers of mine, you did for me' (Matthew 25:40).

Dear Jesus, please remind me to see You in other people and to try to help when they are in difficulty.

*I saw this first in *The Word for Today* published by UCB, but it is found in various forms on the internet.

The Father's tears

How the heart of God must be aching
As He looks upon His world!
Families broken, children starving,
Youth adrift on drugs.
Homes divided, children fatherless ...
A loveless world in chaos.

The tears of God are falling
Upon the reeling world;
And, as He weeps, He longs for hearts
That will watch and weep with Him:
Hearts that will see the brokenness
Where a kingdom of love should be;
Hearts that will hear a Father's voice
Speaking to His children.

He says, 'Look on the world with My eyes,
And, when you do, you will see ...
    Me, in the convict pacing his prison cell,
    Me, in the addict clutching a needle,
    Me, in the prostitute walking dangerous streets,
    Me, in all those who are "other than you",
And your touch on their lives will be My touch.

Will you let your own heart be broken
And care as I have cared?
For then your tears will be mingled with gladness,
As you bring heaven down to earth.'

16. *Fixing our eyes on the horizon*

Imagine yourself standing on the seashore watching a ship sailing towards the horizon. As you keep her in view, she seems to diminish in size, eventually disappearing from your sight. 'She's gone,' you think. And yet you know that she has merely gone from your line of vision. She remains the same ship, size-wise, and those awaiting her arrival on another shore shout, 'She's here!'

I believe that at the moment of death, when the spirit leaves the body, the child of God will be greeted by a welcoming party in heaven exclaiming, 'She's here!' These words of Jesus enable me to believe this – words spoken the night before His own death: 'Let not your heart be troubled. You are trusting God, now trust in me. There are many homes up there where my Father lives, and I am going to prepare them for your coming. When everything is ready, then I will come and get you, so that you can always be with me where I am. If this weren't so, I would tell you plainly' (John 14:1–3, TLB).

The moment of death can be compared to the moment of birth, for whilst in the womb the baby cannot possibly imagine what the parents have planned for his arrival. However, on that arrival, he begins to experience the comforts of the food, the clothes, the cot, the pram and, best of all, the kisses and cuddles; all expressions of his parents' love.

In his letter to the Christians in Corinth, Paul writes, ' ... no mere man has ever seen, heard or even imagined what wonderful things God has ready for those who love the Lord' (1 Corinthians 2:9, TLB).

So what prevents us from being thrilled by the prospect of our heavenly mansion? I have come to believe the truth of this statement: 'The foreground of life can obscure the horizon.' I see 'the foreground of life' as the circumstances in which we find ourselves in our daily lives, some of which we have not chosen – they are the inevitable 'stuff of life'. I think of harrowing sorrows, humdrum duties and surprise joys. Alongside these, we have the experiences resulting from our own desires: those particular things that we always hope will give us pleasure, which may be harmless or even good, when kept in perspective. Yet how easily we can become enmeshed in our circumstances and thereby lose our focus and direction.

As the sailing boat needs the wind to fill its sails and move it on, so *we* need the wind of the Holy Spirit to keep filling us and guiding our voyage to heaven. Will we choose to be led by God's Spirit, keeping our eyes on the horizon, or will we choose to be like children building sandcastles on the seashore? I guess we can all remember our childhood efforts at building the best sandcastles on the beach, only to see them disappear under some trampling feet or beneath the waves of the next tide.

Jesus said, 'All who listen to my instructions and follow them are wise, like a man who builds his house on solid rock ... But those who hear my instructions and ignore them are foolish, like a man who builds his house on sand' (Matthew 7:24,26, TLB).

Jesus, I know that for the joy set before You, You endured the cross. Please help me to allow You to guide me through the circumstances of my life towards that horizon where I will find the place You have prepared for me.

17. Pat

A faithful friend is one of life's greatest blessings. And when a friend has known you for fifty-plus years and has stood with you through life's joys and sorrows, you have a treasure indeed, for such a friend knows your weaknesses and yet still loves you. If that friend shares your love of Jesus then you are truly blessed. Such a friend I had in Pat.

Together with our husbands, Arthur and Cyril, Pat and I had known good times and hard times in the bringing up of our families, but we'd also had the inestimable joy of all four of us accepting Jesus Christ as our Lord and Saviour during the charismatic renewal in the 1970s. Our lives changed as Jesus became the Centre and we had some wonderful, though not easy, years serving the Lord in the ways He led us, individually and as couples. We were each uniquely different and God used us accordingly. Pat's personality was one of love, joy, kindness and enthusiasm. She shone with the love of Jesus.

Then came a hard season when both our husbands died. Within a few more years we both suffered the grief of losing a son. Pat's son, Richard, died suddenly at the age of forty; my son, Paul, died suddenly at the age of forty-two. Through these dark valleys, Pat remained trusting, faithful and loving – always looking outwards to help others.

During the latter years, I'd lived in the South of England and Pat in the North but, though the miles separated us, we kept in touch, seeing each other as often as possible and otherwise chatting on the phone. One such telephone chat took place on 5 September 2009. Pat was her usual cheerful self and I recall, after I'd put down the phone, wondering whether she'd manage to come to me for a little holiday before the autumn arrived. Tragically, that was not to be. Early the following morning, I received a phone call from her daughter to tell me that Pat had died during the night. It seemed unbelievable. She'd been so buoyant, so full of life. My immediate thought was that she must have suffered a heart attack, but later the terrible truth emerged: Pat had been murdered by an intruder, who strangled her then set fire to her home.

One never thinks that such a dreadful thing could happen to someone you know and love. My family and I were deeply shocked and distressed, but our concerns were for Pat's own children and grandchildren.

In my own pain, I turned to God. As I prayed, I received the deep conviction that in that awful moment Jesus, in some way, would have revealed Himself to Pat, and that the revelation would have overridden the horror of what was being done to her. The Holy Spirit brought to mind God's promise, 'I will never leave you or forsake you' (Joshua 1:5), and the words of Jesus Himself, 'Do not be afraid of those who kill the body but cannot kill the soul' (Matthew 10:28). I believe this was confirmed by her neighbour, a doctor, who was allowed to enter her home in the hope that he could help her. Sadly, he could not; but he told the family that he was amazed by the peaceful expression on her face. He thought that, in the circumstances, this was remarkable.

Now, Pat was a lady who often jotted down helpful words and scriptures, so I wasn't surprised when her daughter showed me a piece of paper covered with her recent 'jottings'. I found two of them quite amazing: 'I will take no account of any evil done to me for justice is the Lord's' and 'Seek not the blessings: Seek Him.' These were underlined.

And so, I now thank God for Pat, faithful friend of Jesus and of me, and I give glory to God who, I feel sure, was with her at the end.

Thank You, Jesus, for the gift of friends. Thank You, most of all, that I can call You my Friend – faithful and true, with me in every situation until my dying breath, after which I will see you face to face in the place You are preparing for me.

18. *Heart trouble*

Heart surgery has become almost commonplace but I can still remember how the world seemed to stand still in awe and wonder when the first heart transplant was attempted. Nowadays, I guess most of us know of someone who's had heart surgery, and how thankful they are to have been given a new lease of life – even though that lease will one day expire!

It behoves us all to try to preserve healthy hearts by maintaining a sensible lifestyle. This may involve some sacrifice and discipline. Perhaps we are required to give up smoking, alcohol, cakes or chocolates. And, even though it may go against the grain, we take a walk instead of a car ride. Ultimately, of course, we are the ones who benefit from these good choices for, as the saying goes, 'no pain, no gain'.

That small organ, the heart, is indeed *vital*. When it's functioning as it should, we're unaware of all it's doing for us. But when things begin to go wrong, strange, unpleasant symptoms manifest themselves.

The Bible has much to say about the heart, or the spirit of man. If taken 'to heart', I believe the following words, given to us by our Divine Physician, are the best prescription for a good life:

My son, pay attention to what I say;
listen closely to my words.
Do not let them out of your sight,
keep them within your heart;
for they are life to those who find them
and health to a man's whole body.
Above all else, guard your heart,
for it is the wellspring of life.
(Proverbs 4:20–23)

Our Divine Physician then adds a note to our prescription in Proverbs 17:22:

A cheerful heart is good medicine,
but a crushed spirit dries up the bones.

If our physical hearts need help, we call our doctor and, if we're wise, we heed his advice. Important as that is, it's even more important, in this matter of our spiritual hearts, to take advice from Jesus, our Divine Physician. He's always waiting to hear from us and help us – and we don't have to make an appointment to gain His attention! If He shows us that we need to change our lifestyle, He will also show us how to do this; in fact, He'll deal with us in the way that's perfect for *us*. Just as the physical heart pumps the life-giving blood around our body, so the Holy Spirit fills our yielded hearts with His rivers of 'living water' and we experience God's own love, peace and joy – and, in truth, everything we need to live as God's beloved children.

Thank You, Father, that You have taken away my heart of stone and given me a heart of flesh, so that my desire is to please You and to give You glory.

19. *What's in a name?*

The naming of a child is so important. Before the birth
of each of our babies, Arthur and I spent a great deal of
time pondering the big question, 'What shall this child be
called?' Prospective parents consider numerous factors,
ranging from how a name will sound with the surname,
saints' names and family names, to, quite simply, which
names they like the most.

When I started school at the age of five, answering my
name when Miss Carey called the class register gave me such a
sense of importance. It was the first time I realised that I had a
surname! Until then I'd only known myself as 'Marie'.

Of course, for social and legal reasons it's essential that
we each have a name. As we present our names we present
ourselves, and this is necessary to prove our entitlement to
passports, driving licences and other important documents.
Stealing a person's name and identity is a very serious offence.
So yes, to live in this world we must have a name.

But heaven, too, places a great emphasis on names. In Luke's
Gospel, we read of an angel of the Lord appearing to Zechariah
and saying, 'Your wife Elizabeth will bear you a son, and you
are to *give him the name John*.' Later on we read that the angel
Gabriel was sent by God to Mary to say to her, 'You will ... give
birth to a son, and you are to *give him the name Jesus*.' Still further

on in Luke's Gospel, Jesus said to the seventy-two returning from their first mission, '... rejoice that your *names* are written in heaven' (Luke 1:13,31; 10:20, my emphases).

In the Old Testament, God says to us, 'See, I have written *your name* on the palms of my hands' (Isaiah 49:16, NLT, my emphasis). That verse makes me think of the hands of Jesus as they were pierced by the nails and pinned to a rough wooden cross. Such love! And so the reality is that the names of all who put their trust in Him are then washed in the blood that flows from these wounded hands.

I was prompted to think of these mysteries recently when God revealed something beautiful to me relating to names. It had seemed to me that Mary Magdalene must have loved Jesus passionately, and so I started to pray, 'Jesus, I want to love You the way Mary Magdalene loved You.' Then, one day, I sensed God saying to me, 'I want you to love Me the way only you can love Me. I want *Marie's* love.' Amazing!

As I thought about this, a glimmer of understanding began to dawn. Each one of us is a unique work of our Creator God – our Father. He delights in each one's relationship with Him – each one with a unique personality, history and name. He loves the variety in His children, and watches over our life stories with deep love and interest, waiting for our love offerings – each one different.

I delight in the way my own children show their love for me in different ways. I relish their different personalities which show in the way they love. And this is a reflection of what God showed me when He asked me to love Him as only I can love.

He knows us by name: our names are written in heaven. He delights in our individuality.

Thank You, Lord, that my name is written on the palms of Your hands. May I always hear You when You speak my name and may I respond in love.

20. *From the womb to the tomb*

I wonder why we cannot recall our memories of life in the womb, even though we now know that babies in the womb respond to sounds and happenings around them? Nor do we remember our less than dignified exit from the womb.

And, as for the tomb, I guess that at the end of our lives few of us will qualify for the splendour of a tomb, but no doubt we hope that our bodies will be laid to rest in a respectful way.

This, the lot of every man and every woman, is earthy stuff to consider and reminds me of the words of Job:

> *Naked I came from my mother's womb,*
> *naked I'll return to the womb of the earth.*
> *(Job 1:21, The Message)*

How thankful we should be, therefore, that our lives have a significance far greater than we can ever imagine whilst still in these mortal frames; for, from our birthday to our death day, our choices will decide how we will spend eternity. And the crux is this: how will we respond to Jesus? How will we respond to the cross?

I was once asked, 'Would you become a bee to save the bees?' My instant response was: 'No, I couldn't bear to be a mere insect.' The question had been posed in an effort to help me understand what Jesus had done for me. As I think about it, I'm dumbfounded – that the pure, beautiful Son of God would exchange His heavenly home to dwell in a virgin's womb for nine months and then emerge from it just as all babies do.

I then think of the tomb. Only a dead body is laid in a tomb. The dead body of Jesus bore the marks of His most cruel of deaths – crucifixion.

Jesus chose to be stripped of all dignity both at birth and at death. He was born in poverty in Bethlehem with the purpose of dying in ignominy on Calvary. He chose that journey from womb to tomb so that this proud, selfish human being could be saved from her selfishness and given the assurance of heaven (John 3:16).

His kindness overwhelms me. Was it worth His while? His sacrifice was offered for the sin and guilt of every individual soul, but each person must receive it for him or herself. No one else can do it for us. Indeed, the cross is the crux. Jesus waits to hear our 'Yes'. In the Parable of the Lost Sheep, Jesus says, '... there will be more rejoicing in heaven over one sinner who repents than over ninety-nine righteous persons who do not need to repent' (Luke 15:7).

Jesus, Your humility stops me in my tracks. And You say to me, ' ... learn from me, for I am gentle and humble in heart, and you will find rest for your souls'
(Matthew 11:29).
Please help me to bring my stiff-necked pride to the cross and allow You to be both Saviour and Lord.

21. *The man in the dock*

The perpetrator of a crime knows that, if caught, he will face a public trial and expect to receive a just sentence. But, besides the sentence imposed upon him, he may be carrying within himself painful emotions such as fear, guilt, shame, regret and hopelessness, along with a deep sense of 'aloneness'. No one else can take the punishment for him. He stands alone in the dock.

How sobering it is to realise that 'but for the grace of God' each one of us would be facing a terrible judgment, for we 'all have sinned' blatantly and repeatedly 'and fall short of the glory of God' (Romans 3:23), so we therefore deserve to go on trial and receive God's just sentence. In His pure holiness, God cannot come near to sin, so the only possible just sentence would be eternal separation from Him.

What amazing grace, then, that God Himself in the Person of Jesus, stood in the dock in our place. 'He himself bore our sins in his body on the tree, so that we might die to sins and live for righteousness; by his wounds you have been healed' (1 Peter 2:24). Thus justice was fulfilled, but justice drenched in mercy, for as Romans 8:1 tells us, '... there is now no condemnation for those who are in Christ Jesus'. What a Saviour!

To refuse God's gift of forgiveness is to condemn ourselves to an eternity of separation from God. But to accept Jesus' sacrifice on our behalf means that when the time comes for us to die we will not face judgment for our sins, because His blood has cleansed us from all unrighteousness, and we will spend eternity in heaven with Him.

Let us thank our heavenly Father for His indescribable gift of Jesus.
Let us thank Jesus for dying in our place, that we might go free.
Let us thank the Holy Spirit for staying with us until the day comes when He will lead us home.

22. *The Light of the world*

These are the words of Jesus Himself: 'I am the light of the world. Whoever follows me will never walk in darkness, but will have the light of life' (John 8:12).

There's a beautiful painting in St Paul's Cathedral in London, entitled *The Light of the World*. It's the work of Holman Hunt, and Jesus is shown holding a bright lantern and knocking on a door which is overgrown with brambles and weeds. A strange feature of the door is that it has no handle. That, like everything in the painting, carries an important message based on the words of Jesus above and in the last book of the Bible, 'Here I am! I stand at the door and knock. If anyone hears my voice and opens the door, I will come in and eat with him, and he with me' (Revelation 3:20).

The lantern in Jesus' hand tells us that if we follow Him we will walk in the light. The door symbolises the heart of man. The brambles and weeds speak of the growth in and around our hearts which hinders us opening them to Jesus. And the door handle is on the inside because only *we* can open that door. I guess we all know the things in our own hearts which cause us to hesitate – our own particular sins and weaknesses. Jesus knows them too, which is why He longs to come in and help us.

Jesus' humility and patience amaze me. The One who loved us enough to die for us waits to be invited in; He won't force an entry. When we *do* invite Him in, His Light reveals to us the dark places which we try to hide – even from ourselves – and He shows us how to take the next step of walking in the Light.

Whilst painting this picture, it's said, Hunt himself forsook his agnosticism and was converted to faith in Christ. The painting was taken all over the world and people travelled hundreds of miles to see it. In 1904 it was hung in St Paul's Cathedral. At the service to mark the event, Hunt, now old and almost blind, had to be led out of the cathedral weeping. It's so beautiful the way the presence of Jesus can soften hearts.

Dear Jesus, I open my heart to You and invite You to come in and shine Your light into the places where I have been resistant to You. I am sorry, dear Lord. From now on I want to follow You. Please help me. Thank You for Your humility and patience with me.

Lifting the latch

O God, You are the Light,
Light eternal,
Light that never can be dimmed;
Light that once descended
To a dark and dirty stable,
And now waits silently
To enter into my heart.

O Lord of Light, so humble,
O patient One!
You will not force the door
But wait with longing heart
For me to lift the latch.

Why do I then hold back?
My foolish heart is fearful
That if I let You in
Your light will then reveal
What I don't wish to see.

Yet, if I say, 'Come in!'
You'll enter truly into my dark stable,
And, with Your light, bring peace:
A peace beyond all worldly understanding,
A peace that tells me I am loved
By You, the Light of all the world.

Your kindly light discloses
Only those things I can bear to see
Now, at this moment.
So, let Your light shine in me.
As I surrender to Your Lordship,
Moment by moment, You are changing me.

I lift the latch and bid You enter in.
How blessed I am:
My body has become a temple
For Your indwelling.

23. *The peg bag*

Pocket money was unheard of in our house; years later I understood why. With such a big family as ours, my parents struggled to keep us fed and decently clothed, and they themselves lived truly sacrificial lives.

But let me tell you about the first time I was given a penny to spend. At home, we were always encouraged to recite our newest poem or sing our latest song so, on this occasion, when I was about eight, I said, 'We've learnt the hymn to St George.' 'Let's hear it,' said my father. So dutifully I sang it. Then, to my horror, my parents said, 'Go and sing it for Mrs Robinson.' Now in our home you always obeyed; there was no way I could escape from the hole into which I'd fallen!

Imagine the scene: in our house lived Mum, Dad and six little children; I was the eldest. Next door lived Mr and Mrs Robinson with two teenage daughters. I thought that they were rich and posh – after all, they had a carpet on the floor! What's more, Mrs Robinson had a coat with a big fur collar and her face had a powdered look, which my eight-year-old heart greatly admired. I had a special link with them because, every day after school and on a Saturday morning, I took Mrs Robinson's posh basket to the baker's to get her 'a small brown loaf and three twopenny custards'. At the end of the week, she always gave me threepence, which I immediately gave to Mum. That was taken for granted.

So there I was with the order, 'Go and sing it for Mrs Robinson.' I trembled. How *do* you go to someone's back door, knock, wait and, when it opens, say, 'I've come to sing the hymn to St George for you'? But that is exactly what I had to do. In her kindly way, Mrs Robinson invited me in and I stood in the middle of her room and sang the wretched hymn. That's when she gave me the penny. Then a miracle happened: when I took it home to give to my mother, she said, 'You can keep it.' I couldn't believe my ears – I mean, such a thing had never happened before!

Then came the second miracle, all to do with the penny. As I lay in bed that night, the idea came to me. The following afternoon at school, we'd have Needlework. With my penny, I'd be able to buy a peg bag. This was a piece of coarse material, machine-stitched into a bag shape and with the word 'PEGS' inked across it in large letters. Once you'd done the deal by paying the penny, you stood in a queue and waited for the teacher to thread a needle with the wool of your choice and set you off chain-stitching over the letters. That was what I'd do with my penny.

How the lessons dragged next morning! I was so excited waiting for the afternoon. My determined plan was to buy and embroider the bag in one session and take it home as a big surprise for my mum. All went smoothly until my wool ran out as I approached the end of the word 'PEGS'. Panic filled my heart as I stood in the queue, waiting to have my needle rethreaded. But phew! I made it and, filled with joy, I ran home to give my mum her peg bag.

Why have I told you this simple story? Because I'm touched to think that, as a little child, I wanted to give *all* that I had to my mother. No wonder Jesus tells us that we must become like little children in order to enter the kingdom of heaven.

But what has caused me in later years to become so protective of me and of my possessions? Someone once said, 'A little is a lot if it's all you've got and you give it to Jesus.' I want my heart to love Him so much that, like the child I was, I'm willing to give Him my all. I admit that in this matter I'm still in the School of Learning. One lesson I have learnt: as we accumulate money and possessions, being *over-careful* can cause us to be *full of care*. Another lesson is this: when I'm struggling to be generous in giving, it really does become much easier when I calm myself and, very definitely, say, 'Jesus, I'm giving this to You.' Never to be outdone in generosity He then gives me His peace: He also supplies all my needs.

Lord, my heart says that I want to be childlike and to trust You completely – to really see that everything *I 'have' belongs to You and that I am simply 'minding' it for You. My head says, 'But what if …?' Please help me to practise giving until it becomes natural to me.*

24. *The revolving door*

Just occasionally, in my childhood, I had a glimpse into a different world – a world of luxury. That world was the Corporation Hotel, which in those days was the *only* posh hotel in Middlesbrough. How did *I* enter those hallowed portals? Well, my Auntie Annie was the head waitress there so, to my young girl's mind, she herself was very posh. Sometimes I'd be sent to give a message to Auntie Annie and I made my entrance through a revolving door, which I thought was really exciting. If no one was in sight, my brother and I would steal a few free trips around in this amazing door. Recalling that mini-adventure, I thought: just supposing the doors had contained a mechanism which kept them revolving and we'd been trapped? Fun would quickly have given way to fear and the adventure would have become a nightmare.

Unfortunately, in my own life I've often been trapped in the equivalent of a revolving door. I wonder whether you have? Let me explain. I used to be an inveterate worrier, to the extent that if I realised I wasn't worrying I would worry about what I'd forgotten to worry about! And where did the worry get me? Nowhere! My worried thoughts went over and over the same thing, and I was trapped. This is a ploy of the devil's, which we need to recognise and know how to deal with. Jesus, Himself, says to us, 'Do not *let* your hearts be troubled' (John 14:1, my emphasis) and He also tells us not to keep worrying (Luke 12:29; Matthew 6:25). We are also told in Proverbs to trust in the Lord with all our hearts (Proverbs 3:5). The devil would have us believe that *our* problem is different – too much for God to handle! We have to decide whom we will believe. As someone once said, 'If you pray, why worry? And if you worry, why bother praying?'

So, how do I deal with the 'revolving door syndrome' of worry? I ask God to show me if there's anything I should do in the particular situation, and I try to do it. I then ask Him to help me to relinquish it all to Him and I thank Him for looking after it. I find a scripture verse that helps me and I speak it out. Hebrews 4:12 tells us that the Word of God is alive and active and can pierce between the soul (our mind and heart) and the spirit. I have found that to be true: as I focus on His Word, peace comes to my mind and heart.

Of course there are many other 'revolving door syndromes' – different things for different people – but the way to deal with them is always the same. Jesus came to set the captive free. The choice is ours – but how thankful I am that Jesus understands our struggles and our weaknesses, and is always waiting, with compassion, to help us up when we fall. His mercies are new every morning; and sometimes these mercies come to us through people standing with us to help, and supporting us in counsel and prayer.

Dear Lord, please help me to recognise when my mind and emotions are trapped in a continuous cycle. May I have the wisdom to use Your Word and defeat the devil's plans. Thank You that You came to set the captive free.

25. *The mystery tour*

I'd decided to explore the possibility of a coach tour holiday. After my initial enquiry, the brochures began to arrive thick and fast. It intrigued me that they all advertised 'Mystery Tours', which carried the following request: 'Do not ask your driver for the final destination because even he doesn't know where he's going.' Whoops! Now that didn't appeal to me at all, as I visualised myself arriving at a place I'd *never* have chosen for a holiday. I knew that I'd want to be sure of my final destination and also that the driver would know where he was going!

It occurred to me that there are similarities between the 'Mystery Tour' and the 'Journey of Life', which at times is a mystery to us. We can be deeply puzzled and hurt by inexplicable happenings, such as a serious accident, the loss of work, sickness, early death, a broken marriage ... So many things can cause us to ask: 'Why is this happening to me?' At other times, we may experience great joys, as in marriage, a baby's birth, friendships or family celebrations. Again we may wonder, 'Why am I so blessed?' and think, 'I don't deserve this, but I'm *so* grateful'. Then, of course, there are the seasons in life's journey which are simply humdrum and we wonder why our lives are so dull.

So yes, there is mystery on life's journey, much of which will not be understood until we reach our final destination. But surely, the greatest mystery is that God Himself is with us on our journey, if we have surrendered our lives to Him, allowing Him to be the driver. He is with us in the midst of the sorrows, the joys and the humdrum but, unlike the coach driver, Jesus knows where He's taking us. As He comforted His disciples on the eve of His crucifixion, He said, 'In my Father's house are many rooms … I am going there to prepare a place for you … I will come back and take you to be with me that you also may be where I am' (John 14:2–3).

Often, when praying, I feel moved to exclaim, 'I am caught up in the Mystery' – the Mystery of Father, Son and Holy Spirit, all deeply involved in 'little' me and my journey through life.

So this we know: believers in Christ can be sure of their final destination. When the time comes, our faithful driver will watch over our safe arrival. As He has promised: 'Never will I leave you; never will I forsake you' (Hebrews 13:5).

Dear Jesus, please help me to allow You to be in the driving seat as I journey through life with its many mysteries. Thank You that You are utterly trustworthy and faithful.

26. 'I'm not ready for this yet'

Time was slipping by. The years seemed to pass ever more quickly and the realisation came that I should grasp the nettle and write my will. I therefore contacted a firm which specialises in 'Will Writing' and made the necessary appointment.

I had an interesting conversation with the gentleman who came to advise me. He told me that very many people shy away from performing this task which necessarily compels us to face the stark reality of our mortality. On one occasion, following a talk he'd given about writing one's will, a gentleman said, 'I'm not ready for this yet.' He was ninety-two!

This brought to mind my recent holiday. It was my first experience of cruising. I know that many people thoroughly enjoy the cruise-ship lifestyle, as is evidenced by the number of cruises they fit into a year. However, the whole experience left me feeling distinctly uneasy. Never before had I been so pampered: the food, drink, entertainment and service were lavish, but I learnt that the hard-working waiters were paid a pittance and were dependent upon generous gratuities from the passengers in order to send money home to their struggling families in the Philippines. To me, this seemed all wrong and I felt very sorry for them.

But, as the week went by, I began to feel a real concern for the passengers, most of whom were retired; some, indeed, were very elderly. I wondered how many of them were like the ninety-two-year-old – unable to face the fact that death is the inevitable last stage of life on this earth, and so they fill their days with pleasurable distractions. Such people are poorer than the poor waiters, I thought, and one can understand them seeking every possible pleasure – for life without hope must be very hard.

Thank God for Jesus who came from heaven to give us a living hope. In his letter to the Thessalonians, Paul writes, 'Since Jesus died and broke loose from the grave, God will most certainly bring back to life those who died in Jesus' (1 Thessalonians 4:14, *The Message*). And a beautiful verse from the Psalms says, 'When they arrive at the gates of death, GOD welcomes those who love Him' (Psalm 116:15, *The Message*).

How amazing that God Himself will welcome us, His children. Let us hold on to His promises, remembering further words from Paul: 'If we died with him, we will also live with him; if we endure, we will also reign with him' (2 Timothy 2:11–12).

Thank You, Jesus, that in Your own life You demonstrated that death is not the end. Please help me to live my life, trusting in Your promises.

27. *Keep looking to Him*

'Turn to me and be saved, all you ends of the earth; for I am God, and there is no other' (Isaiah 45:22).

When my grandson Sam was four I often took him to school. Holding hands, we'd walk the meandering, uphill pathway from the school gate right up to his classroom door. One morning, however, his four-year-old cousin, David, was with us. To my surprise, once through the school gate, Sam said to David, 'Let's run,' and, leaving my side, they set off at a trot. How small and vulnerable they looked amongst the older, stronger children! I was amazed by this display of courage – no longer the timid little boy, he was brave as a lion!

An interesting thing then happened for, as he came to the first bend in the path, he stopped, looked back and, ensuring that I was still there, continued on the marathon. This happened at every turn in the path. I was impressed by his good sense, for he saw me as his security and, while I could be kept in view, he felt safe.

What a lesson for me! Surely I too should be so conscious of my need of God's presence that I keep looking to Him – at every turn in my day. It's a most wonderful truth that there is not a single moment of my life when God is not waiting for me to turn my mind and heart to Him. And just as Sam's confidence in me delighted my heart, the heart of my heavenly Father delights in my childlike trust in Him. When I allow the following words to seep into my heart, I know God's presence and peace …

I AM

I was regretting the past
And fearing the future.

Suddenly, my Lord spoke to me:
'My name is I AM.'

He paused, and I waited;
Then He continued:

'When you visit the past
With its mistakes and regrets,
It is hard: I am not there.
My name is not I WAS!

'When you live in the future
With its problems and fears,
It is hard: I am not there.
My name is not I WILL BE!

'When you live in this moment
With all it holds,
It is not *hard: for I am here.*
My name is I AM!'

Thank You, Lord, for Your faithfulness to me. I am humbled as I realise how often I am unfaithful to You. You who once said that You have come so that we might have life and have it more abundantly (John 10:10), help me to live in this present moment in the awareness and peace of Your holy presence.

28. 'We've found the cross'

Losing something is always upsetting. I well remember the time I lost something very precious to me. I discovered its loss during a prayer meeting, as my hand wandered to my neck and, to my great consternation, I realised that my cross and chain were missing. How I struggled to focus on the prayer. As soon as the meeting ended, I blurted out my great loss – for great loss it was, being a memento of my only visit to the Holy Land, a visit made possible through the generosity of my son, Paul. For me it had great sentimental value.

My friends sprang into action: the hunt was on, but it soon became clear that my cross and chain were not in the house. However, as we were leaving, the light of a torch caught a gleam of gold on the floor of the porch. Alas, it revealed only the chain. There was no sign of the cross and I returned home feeling very sad.

Imagine my delight and gratitude, therefore, when the following day my host of the previous evening rang me to say, 'We've found the cross!' He'd asked his children to go out in the daylight and search for it. They'd found it in the lay-by in which we'd parked our car. It had lain there unnoticed for twenty-four hours.

'Unnoticed!' How blessed we are to be living in a land where the cross *can* be freely displayed: I pray that it will always be so. But that night I was challenged to ask myself this question: 'Do I notice the cross?' There it is, atop our churches; there it is, woven into our national flag; and there it is, freely worn by so many, yet how rarely do I actually notice it. 'Familiarity breeds contempt' goes the saying. I cannot bear to think of being contemptuous of the cross but I was brought to the realisation that I should be much more sensitively aware of a cross when I see one.

For surely, the purpose of these crosses is to remind us of the gallows on which the Son of God willingly gave His life as a sacrifice for the sin of the whole world. Therefore, the truth is that each one of us can say: 'He did it for me.' Perhaps, then, when we notice a cross, our instinctive heart response could be a simple prayer: 'You did it for me; thank You, Jesus.'

Sadly, there are many places in the world where Christians do not have the freedom to display signs of their faith. Many are willing to suffer persecution, even death, rather than deny Jesus. So perhaps our prayer could be followed by one for those who are being persecuted.

'We've found the cross,' said my friend. How blessed we are if we have found *the cross*, for in so doing we've found the forgiveness, love and peace only Jesus can give.

Dear Jesus, thank You for the cross. I cannot imagine the horror of Your deathbed. Not for You a comfortable bed surrounded by caring people. Your deathbed was of rough wood, in a vertical rather than horizontal position. Nails pinned Your body to the wood. No caring hands comforted You. You were, and are, my only hope of heaven. Thank You, Jesus, for the cross.

The blood of Jesus

Only through the blood of Jesus
Am I cleansed from all my sin.
Only through the blood of Jesus
Can I enter in.

His holy blood has justified me,
His holy blood has sanctified me.
It's through His blood that I'm redeemed,
And through His blood that I am healed.

Thank You for Your blood, O Jesus,
Now upon the mercy seat.
Thank You for Your Son, O Father;
The offering perfect and complete.

Holy Spirit, You have led me
To the gateway of the cross,
Now with all my heart I thank You,
Father, Son and Holy Ghost.

29. *The news*

For many, reading the morning newspaper is as essential as having a shower or eating breakfast. You could say that they're hungry for the news of the moment.

I remember an occasion, some years ago, when I needed to get to our local post office and newsagent's by 9am, so I set off early to walk along the narrow footpath which was the most direct route. To my surprise, I kept meeting people already returning from the shop. It was obvious that the reason for their early start was their need to get the morning paper. In fact, several of them, unable to wait until they reached home, were reading it as they walked along. I had to do a smart sidestep to avoid a collision with one lady, so immersed was she in reading her newspaper!

Of course we need to keep up with the news, even though we know that the day's headlines are often bad news. The nature of news is that it's new – sometimes good, sometimes bad; sometimes important, sometimes unimportant. And, just occasionally, we receive news which changes our lives: hearing of the birth of a baby or the death of a loved one. But mostly what is 'news' today is soon forgotten.

How truly remarkable therefore that a news item announced over 2,000 years ago is still a 'top story' which has been, and continues to be, life-changing 'good news'. The news item to which I refer was transmitted from heaven to earth on the night of the birth of Jesus in Bethlehem. It was delivered by an angel to shepherds in a field. The angel said them, "'Do not be afraid. I bring you good news of great joy that will be for all the people. Today in the town of David a Saviour has been born to you; he is Christ the Lord. This will be a sign to you: You will find a baby wrapped in cloths and lying in a manger." Suddenly a great company of the heavenly host appeared with the angel, praising God and saying, "Glory to God in the highest, and on earth peace to men on whom his favour rests"' (Luke 2:10–14).

Many scoff at that news, seeing it as little more than a fairy story; but for those who believe, it proves to be the very best of news. It's reported for us in the Bible, that wonderful book which is the story of our redemption from Genesis to Revelation. For me, it's essential to read the 'good news' in the Bible every day.

So I keep abreast with the news of the day but I endeavour to hold it in perspective, filtering it through the Word of God: 'Your word is a lamp to my feet and a light for my path' (Psalm 119:105).

Thank You, Jesus, that You are the Word made flesh. You came to bring good news to the poor. Help me to realise how poor I am and how much I need You.

30. *The 'good' person's problem*

I really was a *good* little girl – everyone said so! As I was the eldest of nine children, much was expected of me and I tried to live up to expectations. It was impressed upon me that I should be a good example to my younger siblings. So, I was obedient and tried to keep all the rules at home, school and church – and, believe me, there were many rules!

Another of my childhood virtues was that I was very helpful to my mother. Fear had prompted obedience, but my helpfulness came from a real desire to ease my mother's load. Her work was endless and she always looked tired, so I did what I could to help.

Alongside all this helping and rule-keeping, I had a deep fear of failing at school because it would bring such disappointment to my parents and shame upon me. So, I worked very hard at my studies – and, yes, I was a good little girl!

The years passed and I grew up to be a good big girl, a good young woman and a good wife and mother. I kept the rules as well as I possibly could. Church attendance and the recital of many prayers were a central part of my life, because this was what was expected; but also because I had been brought up to believe that I had to *earn* my salvation through prayer and good works. And so I did all I could to book a place in heaven! Looking back, I can see what a dutiful but joyless life

I was living. Sadly, it never occurred to me that there might be another way.

My release came in the 1970s by means of a wonderful outpouring of God's Holy Spirit on His Church, known as the 'charismatic renewal'. Through good, Bible-based teaching, light began to dawn. For the first time, I heard that God, my Father, loves *me* personally and cares about every detail of my life. He loves me as much as He loves His beloved Son, Jesus. Jesus' life here on earth, ending with His cruel death on a cross in my place, convinced me of this amazing love. So, now all the striving could end. I simply had to learn how to rest in that love.

The next important truth I learnt was that however 'good' I was, I couldn't *earn* my salvation. The sinless Jesus, who came to save the world, died on the cross for the sin of all the world. He, therefore, *is* my salvation and I can only go to God through Him. 'I am the way and the truth and the life. No-one comes to the Father except through me' (John 14:6) – Jesus' own words!

The choice was mine. After a lifetime of being 'the good one', would I be able to accept that I am, in reality, a sinner and that my 'goodness' cannot stand before the eyes of a holy, holy, holy God? Good people often struggle in this situation, listing the good deeds they've done and the evil they've avoided. To admit to a *need* for Jesus comes hard. Interestingly, and perhaps understandably, criminals, whose sins are known to themselves and others, often accept the 'good news' more readily. Deeply thankful and full of joy, they begin to live dramatically changed lives. Recognising their own unworthiness, they have no false pride to conquer.

However, I was not left alone to make this choice. God gave me the grace to see and to accept His love and forgiveness. My own experience brought about a gradual change in my life and I am so grateful to God for His love, mercy and patience. The motive for my actions changed from duty to love, and I still thank God every day for this new life. God loves me. He longs for me to love Him and His Holy Spirit guides and empowers me to live this new life through Jesus. It really is a love affair – 'the divine romance'. That step of faith and humility at the foot of the cross transfers us from the kingdom of darkness into the kingdom of God's beloved Son.

Father God, thank You for making the way for me, a helpless sinner, to come into Your holy Presence through the blood of Jesus.

I am the gate

There is a gate to Father's House,
And that gateway is Jesus,
Who says to all, 'Come in through Me.
No other way will lead you.

'So many are the offers
Attracting eager minds,
Drawing on eyes and ears and hearts
With an artifice that blinds.

'Yet here I stand, faithful and true,
With open arms and heart,
Waiting for you to enter in
And never more depart.

'Once through this holy gateway
The treasures you will find
Are perfect love and peace and life;
All else you'll leave behind.

'Your joy will be to please your God,
To worship at His throne,
When you enter through that narrow gate
That leads you to your home.'

31. *The birthday party*

I'll always remember the tenth birthday party of my son, Richard, for at that party I learnt a salutary lesson.

I wanted the party to go really well, of course, and nothing was overlooked in my preparations. Being a schoolteacher, I rather prided myself on my ability to manage children; so, bringing my skills and experience to bear, I had a good programme of games arranged for before and after the birthday tea.

All went according to plan until we finished tea, when I suddenly decided to deviate slightly from *my* programme. I suggested to Richard that he could take the boys into the garden to play whilst I cleared away the tea things. They raced outside as though released from prison! I stood at the kitchen sink and gazed out upon the scene. We had several large trees in the garden. Without exception, the boys were, like monkeys, climbing the trees and having a great time. Seeing them so happy, I abandoned my own 'good ideas' and allowed them to play their own games in freedom. They were released and so was I!

It was a good party. The boys enjoyed their games and they enjoyed the food, but it also gave *me* food for thought. How often do we exhaust ourselves doing unnecessary things? Our own 'good ideas' sometimes prove to be not such good ideas after all.

In those days I didn't realise that God's Holy Spirit would guide me in making decisions, both big and small. It's an amazing truth that God says, '... I know the plans I have for you ... plans to prosper you and not to harm you, plans to give you hope and a future' (Jeremiah 29:11). Seeking His will for our lives is true wisdom, for 'Unless the LORD builds the house, its builders labour in vain' (Psalm 127:1).

It is helpful to take stock from time to time, asking ourselves how we *do* spend our time, writing down the things we know are essential and then listing all our other activities.

Wouldn't it be beautiful to be able to say that everything we do is done from the purest of motives! Some of us strive for perfection or to gain approval. For others, guilt or fear of condemnation might instead be the driving force. For some, busyness is an attempt to escape from ourselves and from reality. And yet others of us allow people to manipulate us. When we allow any of these factors to motivate our actions we lose our way and our peace.

Thankfully, we can ask the Holy Spirit to guide us through our heart-searching and then to help us discern what God would have us do. He certainly wants us to have time for our own needs to be met.

Jesus lived the perfectly balanced life. Everything flowed from the time He spent with Father God and He is our model. I believe that God gives me peace of heart when I am doing what He would have me do. 'Who, then, is the man that fears the LORD? He will instruct him in the way chosen for him' (Psalm 25:12).

Help me, Lord, to start each day by abandoning myself to You, and then may I trust You to lead and guide me in my choices.

32. *The 'sat nav'*

Technology, to me, is a mystery. When I first experienced the wonders of a 'sat nav' it was easy for me to picture it as a kindly person up in the sky, guiding us on our way – her voice so sure, so precise, firmly compelling us to obey exactly, if we wanted to reach our destination. What a comfort such a device would have been to me in my driving days, for I always lived in fear of losing the way when going somewhere new.

On that first magical journey with our admittedly rather bossy navigator, I was with my daughter, Miriam, and her husband, Stuart, en route to the London home of their daughter, Rachel. Door to door, the journey was perfectly accomplished. Quite marvellous!

However, on another occasion, I was travelling with friends to an area of Devon which was new to them. No worries – we had our friend the 'sat nav'! We obediently followed every instruction with complete confidence. We had no doubts: the 'sat nav' *must* be right. And, of course, it was, because we did indeed eventually reach our destination – but only after negotiating a most tortuous and hazardous route. We learnt, on our arrival, that there was a much easier, alternative way. As I sat in the back of the car, free of all responsibility, the thought came to me that since we so readily obey the sat nav's instructions, putting our complete faith and trust in it, why can't we be like that with the directions God gives us for the journey of life?

The Bible has been termed, 'The Maker's Handbook', and I do believe that we can find direction in God's Word for every situation in life. As we read earlier, Psalm 119:105 declares: 'Your word is a lamp to my feet and a light for my path.' In my own life I've found that when I choose to obey God's Word I experience peace in my heart. Sadly, I sometimes forget or choose to ignore His direction and then I find myself wandering along 'tortuous and hazardous paths' until I come to my senses. Then, how humbled I feel when I find my Good Shepherd waiting to help me back onto the right road.

Here's a thought-provoking story. A young ensign in the US Navy was given the opportunity to show his ability to get a ship out of port. In the US Navy an ensign is a commissioned officer of the lowest rank. This ambitious young officer had the decks buzzing with men and he actually set a new record for getting the destroyer under way. Such success – until he received this message from the Captain: 'My personal congratulations on completing the exercise according to the book and with amazing speed. *However*, in your haste you have overlooked one of the unwritten rules: make sure the Captain is on board before getting under way.' Ouch!

The question we need to ask ourselves is: have we got Jesus on board as we journey though life? His desire is to guide us by His Word and by His Spirit. His directions are sure and He longs to lead us on the best roads. How wise we are if we listen to His voice and obey Him!

Please help me, Lord, to realise how blessed I am to have Your Word and Your Spirit to direct me. Why do I first run for guidance to people or to books? Help me to choose to spend quiet time each day alone with You so that I can confidently expect Your word of direction; for I know that without You, Jesus, as my Captain, I am lost.

33. Coincidence or 'God-incidence'?

During a period of my life I frequently took a bus from Winchester to Romsey, in order to visit my sister in a nursing home. I was often aware of a gentleman doing the same bus journey.

One day, whilst waiting in the bus shelter, this gentleman was sitting next to me. We got into conversation. I told him I'd been visiting my sister and he showed real kindness and concern. One thing led to another and, by the time the bus arrived, we were talking about my book, *As Time Goes By*, which had just been published.

We boarded the bus and he took a seat near to me so that conversation was still possible. After a short while, I sensed that the Holy Spirit was nudging me to offer him a copy of my book. The thought wouldn't go away so, rather sheepishly, I asked him if he'd like one. He was totally delighted, the more so when I offered to inscribe it. This I managed to do at the next bus stop, having first ascertained that his name was John.*

He then went on to tell me about a female neighbour who was a Christian. 'Where does she worship?' I asked. 'Christ Church,' was his reply. As I too worship in Christ Church, my next question was, 'What's her name?' His answer stunned me: his neighbour was my prayer partner of many years. Not only that but, over the years, from time to time she had asked if we could pray for her neighbour, John.* And there he was, the pleased possessor of my book. I prayed that he would be blessed by it.

Coincidence? I don't think so; for when we pray God is always working to bring about His purposes in the lives of the people for whom we pray. Sadly, we can fail to recognise and obey His promptings. And sadly, too, we can fail to acknowledge His clever arranging of people and situations and so we do not give Him the thanks He deserves. I think we should try to recognise and obey His promptings in little things, so that this becomes a way of life. And if we don't always get it right – well, it's all right to make a mistake. The one who never made a mistake, never did anything!

I know that I have a long way to go in developing this way of thinking, but of one thing I am sure: each time I respond to His gentle promptings, it delights His Father heart. And that is true for all of us.

* Name changed

O Lord, as I abandon myself to You, I believe that You engineer my circumstances. Please help me to see You in the people I meet and to serve You in them.

34. *Money*

'True generosity is this: you give your all, and yet, you always feel as if it costs you nothing.' So wrote Simone de Beauvoir. When I read that, I felt myself squirming. I'm in the kindergarten in this 'School of Learning'.

In 1946, a widowed mother was struggling to bring up her three teenage children. Times were hard yet, despite their many deprivations, this mother had made their home a truly happy place and they were contented.

As the feast of Easter approached, their pastor asked his small congregation to make a sacrifice and save up towards a special Easter offering for a needy family. The mother and her children went home and started to plan: they would live on the most basic food – just bread and potatoes; they would go to bed early and save on coal and lamplight; they would walk to school and the shops instead of getting on buses. And the three children would all try to earn a bit of money by babysitting.

When Easter Sunday came, they went to church feeling excited and rich with £16 to put in the offering for the 'needy family'. The shock came later in the day when their pastor arrived at their home, bringing them the gift of the Easter offering. *They* were the needy family! It was a sobering moment. They had not felt at all 'needy'. Indeed, they'd felt like millionaires as they gave away their hard-earned £16! But they could not be ungracious and refuse the gift, so they waited for guidance.

The following Sunday, a visiting missionary to their church made an appeal for money towards the £75 it would cost to replace his church roof in Africa. Mum drew an envelope from her purse. It contained £65 – the gift they had received as the 'needy family'. It passed from one to the other of the teenagers and, with real joy, they put it in the offering for Africa. 'You must have some rich people in this church,' said the delighted missionary to the pastor. I think he had!

One day when Jesus observed people putting their money into the Temple treasury, He saw that the rich threw in large amounts but a poor widow put in two very small copper coins, worth only a fraction of a penny. He said to His disciples, 'I tell you the truth, this poor widow has put more into the treasury than all the others. They all gave out of their wealth; but she, out of her poverty, put in everything – all she had to live on' (Mark 12:43–44).

A little is a lot if it's all you've got and you give it to Jesus.

Heavenly Father, help me to remember that every good gift comes from You. Please help me to use everything You give me in the way that delights Your heart.

35. *Launch into the deep*

There are depths in us which no one sees but God and ourselves. Who can plumb the depths of our hearts? Only God and we ourselves – if we dare!

It takes courage to plumb those depths because we're afraid to face the things we've buried. These could be sins, weaknesses, wrong desires or wrong attitudes. Jeremiah 17:9–10 tells us that the human heart is deceitful, even mortally sick and that the Lord Himself searches our minds and hearts. We feel afraid that people would be shocked if they could see us as we really are, deep within. What a comfort it is to know that God does see all our buried 'toxic waste' and yet He still loves us. He longs to set us free and heal us. To me, at my time of life, another great comfort is that we're never too old to change!

Alfred Nobel became a rich man through his invention of dynamite and other explosives. When his brother died, a newspaper made the embarrassing mistake of printing the wrong obituary – Alfred's! He was shocked to read the stark truth that he'd become wealthy through enabling people to kill each other in unprecedented numbers. This revelation brought him to a crossroads in his life. He could choose to ignore this insight and continue in the same way; he could sink helplessly into depression and guilt; or he could use his great wealth for the good of humanity. There must have been some deep heart-searching. Thankfully, he chose the last of these options and thus was born the Nobel Peace Prize.

It must be a weird experience to read one's own obituary. As I thought about it, I began to wonder how my own obituary would read if written, not by a newspaper reporter, but by the hand of God. After all, He *does* know all the facts: 'O LORD, you have searched me and you know me … you perceive my thoughts from afar' (Psalm 139:1–2). How terrible it would be to read in this obituary: 'She would never let us plumb the depths together and therefore never fulfilled My vision for her life. Some doors in her heart were kept firmly locked and to My great sadness, she never experienced the freedom, fruitfulness and growth in ability I had planned for her.' That would surely be so sad!

For almost half my life it never occurred to me that I needed to change, or that change was possible. I went to Confession regularly and every time I confessed to the same old litany of sins. My life began to change when the truth of the gospel broke through into my heart. It was a moment of revelation, just as reading his own obituary had been for Alfred Nobel. It became clear to me that Jesus had come to take away the sins of the whole world, including mine. I was so grateful to know this – and that gratitude grows day by day. The Holy Spirit lives in me, comforting me and guiding me. My heavenly Father loves me. In truth I often say, 'I'm caught up in the Mystery.'

In the enterprise of 'plumbing the depths' I find it a great help to have someone to whom I can be accountable. For many years I've met once a week with a friend who is my prayer partner. We meet to share and pray and, as we've grown to know and trust each other, we can confess our weaknesses and failures as we pray with and for each other. This is a great blessing.

Surrendering to God the hidden things we'd rather not face up to is the journey of transformation – being changed into His likeness. It is the very purpose of 'our being' and will be ongoing until we see Him face to face.

Jesus, You are the Light of the world. I need Your Light to shine into the deep recesses of my very being, allowing You to reveal to me the things which need to change. Please help me to recognise Your gentle prompting and then willingly submit to whatever You ask of me.

36. *Arrivals*

I'd been visiting my son, Richard, Maria, my daughter-in-law, and their children and was returning home by train. We arrived at the railway station. Standing in the prime parking place was a large limousine. The chauffeur was whiling away the waiting time by polishing the car, removing every last speck of dust. Nearby stood policemen and a reception committee. We wondered which VIP would emerge from the train!

As the time for the expected arrival drew near, all the men moved to their designated positions. It was then that I overheard someone say, 'It's the Foreign Secretary.' He alighted from the train and everyone jumped into action to get him safely into the waiting limousine. How impressive it all seemed!

Of course it is right and good to give honour where honour is due, but let's always remember to give honour, first and foremost, to God. Psalm 8 expresses this for us:

> *O LORD, our Lord,*
> *how majestic is your name in all the earth!*
> *... When I consider your heavens,*
> *the work of your fingers,*
> *the moon and the stars,*
> *which you have set in place,*
> *what is man that you are mindful of him,*
> *the son of man that you care for him?*

You made him a little lower than the heavenly beings
and crowned him with glory and honour. (Psalm 8:1,3–5)

Witnessing the arrival of the Foreign Secretary caused me to think about 'arrivals'. They are, of course, part and parcel of life. Expectant parents endeavour to have everything ready for the arrival of their baby. A family member, arriving home after a long absence, will be greeted by a welcoming party at the airport, to be followed by a celebration of their return. Move up the social scale and consider a royal visit. No detail is overlooked in preparation for a visit from the Queen.

But what of the arrival of Jesus on this planet? This had been foretold 400 years before, by the prophet Isaiah. 'Therefore the LORD himself will give you a sign: The virgin will be with child and will give birth to a son, and will call him Immanuel' (Isaiah 7:14). Yes, the Jewish nation was waiting for Messiah to arrive, yet when He came as a helpless baby His arrival went almost unnoticed.

However, we can be certain that when Jesus comes again His arrival will be seen by all as He Himself prophesied: 'Then, the Arrival of the Son of Man! It will fill the skies – no one will miss it. Unready people all over the world … will raise a huge lament as they watch the Son of Man blazing out of heaven … The Arrival of the Son of Man will take place in times like Noah's. Before the great flood everyone was carrying on as usual, having a good time right up to the day Noah boarded the ark. They knew nothing – until the flood hit and swept everything away. The Son of Man's arrival will be like that ...' (Matthew 24:30–31,37–39, *The Message*).

Jesus went on to tell several parables, all with the same message: 'Be prepared.' So, how can we be prepared? The first step is to turn to Jesus, repent of our sins and receive His forgiveness. The next step is to surrender our lives to Him, allowing Him to be the Centre. His Holy Spirit will then come and live in us to guide and strengthen us.

When the time comes for Jesus to return, it will be a day of great rejoicing for all who have received Him as Saviour and Lord. But for those who've refused Him entrance into their lives, it will be a day of terrible mourning. Let us resolve to be like the wise virgins in Jesus' parable – prepared and alert.

Dear Jesus, please help me to be wise in the way I live, knowing that You could return at any time. Maranatha, come, Lord Jesus.

My chair

I hadn't realised,
I hadn't understood;
The habit so ingrained,
I'd usurped the place of God
In my little life.

For I'd grown so used
To seeing others' faults,
To criticising in my heart
And often in my talk
In my little life.

And then one day
Just like a lightning bolt
The awful truth struck home:
I was seated on a chair
I'd fashioned for myself,
Moulded to my shape –
So comfortable,
My judgment seat.

Oh, how my heart was smitten!
At once I saw that
There can be
Only one Judge,
The Lord.
Only one Judgment Seat,
The Lord's.
He is the One who says,
'Be merciful
As your Father in heaven
Is merciful.
Judge not
And you shall not
Be judged.'
Out of my depths I cry,
'Have mercy, Lord,
Have mercy,
Oh Lord, have mercy on me.'

How dreadful it would be
If, hardening His heart,
He coldly answered,
'No.'
Imagine my despair,
My devastation.
Impossible to bear
Such desolation.

But such is not my fate.
Thank You, dear Lord,
For all Your mercies to me.
And, Holy Spirit, help me
To be more and more uncomfortable
On my self-made judgment seat
In this, my little life.

37. 'Without the stuff, I'm nothing'

'Without the stuff, I'm nothing.' Those words were spoken to Joel Edwards when he was working as a probation officer. The speaker was nineteen years of age – a clever thief who always wore the very best in clothes and jewellery. The statement was his response to Joel's question, 'Why do you spend so much money on these things?' Swift as an arrow came that reply, 'Without the stuff, I'm nothing.' How very sad! Joel admitted that he could never forget it. Nor can I.

It's all too easy for anyone to fall into that way of thinking. Clever advertising can convince us that a particular product is essential if we desire to be accepted and successful. The dangled carrot can be anything from make-up and clothes through to the 'dream house' and car. Now, whilst these things are not harmful in themselves, the danger comes when we find that we must have them to boost our self-esteem. Sadly, when we get onto that treadmill, we're likely to wear ourselves out in order to gain something which will quickly become outmoded and valueless.

A poor self-image does *not* come from God. In Genesis chapter 1 we read that God made man in His own image: male and female He created them. God looked over all He had made and saw that it was very good. The psalmist understood this when he exclaimed to God, 'Thank you for making me so wonderfully complex! … Your workmanship is marvelous – and how well I know it' (Psalm 139:14, TLB).

It is indeed a great feeling to know that something we've made or achieved is very good. Our gifts vary and so, therefore, do our accomplishments. If we've baked a delicious cake, built a splendid house or performed a beautiful piece of music (there are as many possible achievements as there are people), we know what it feels like to be satisfied with our workmanship. Surely that must be a very pale reflection of how God feels about us. God made us and He loves us. From beginning to end, the Bible expresses God's love for us. 'Can a mother forget her little child and not have love for her own son? Yet even if that should be, I will not forget you' (Isaiah 49:15, TLB). If we truly believed that, we would not compare ourselves with others and our possessions with theirs. We would rest content in the knowledge that our heavenly Father is watching over us. The psalmist says, 'Where is the man who fears the Lord? God will teach him how to choose the best' (Psalm 25:12, TLB).

Satan is God's enemy and our enemy, too. His ploy is to sow seeds of doubt into our minds as he did with Eve in the Garden of Eden. We find ourselves wondering, 'Did God *really* say that?' The enemy's tactics do not change, so we should be prepared: the mind is the battleground. When a thought which denies God's Word comes into our minds, we should replace it with the truth and, if possible, speak out the appropriate verse from the Bible, thus declaring what God has said about us. As our confidence in God grows we will come to the place of being able to say, 'Even without "the stuff" I am someone of precious worth to my heavenly Father.'

Dear Lord, please help me to believe that You made me in Your own image. You called me by name and I am known to You. How precious are Your works! Therefore I am precious. I choose to believe what You say about me and to reject the negative statements which undermine and damage me.

The gift of God's love

We'd listened to a beautiful sermon about God's love for us. But, even as I marvelled at such bounty, I had a sense that many people feel unable to receive that love because they're locked in their pasts. In their minds they see themselves clothed in the tattered garments of guilt, regret, disappointment, hurt or other negative things: this makes them feel unable to approach God and receive His gifts.

To all who feel like that, He says:

Come, My child. I hold out My hands and ask you to give your past to Me. I know all that has happened in your life. I was there and I am here, now. Entrust it all to Me. Let it rest with Me. I love you. I wait for you. As you come to Me, repent of your sins and receive My forgiveness. I will remove your tattered robe and clothe you in My robe of righteousness. I long to hold you close to My heart that you may feel My love. The past is gone. Let us rejoice together.

38. *Wrapped up in self*

'He's so wrapped up in himself.' We've all heard, and perhaps used, that expression; an expression which can, of course, be used equally to describe a man or a woman.

Wrapped up in self. For me, that conjures up a picture of someone all bound up in layers of adhesive tape, unable to look around or move from one position. How awful, I think, to be so restricted, so self-absorbed! A person wrapped up in 'self' makes a very small parcel. But then I have to stop and pose the question: 'Could that possibly describe me?' Perhaps I don't appear to others to be wrapped up in myself and I may not be aware of the layers of self-love that bind me. *But* I know that, if I am to be free, God and I together must get below those layers and peel them away.

Many of us, I'm sure, remember playing the party game of 'Pass the parcel'. Standing in a circle while the music played, we would pass a bulkily-wrapped parcel from one to another. When the music stopped, whoever was holding the parcel had to remove one layer of the paper. The music then resumed and so the game continued, a layer of paper being removed each time the music stopped. Whoever was holding the parcel when the final layer came off won the prize which had been hidden beneath all those layers.

As I think of this game and of the many layers of paper, I can compare them to the layers of selfishness I've discovered in myself. I'm shocked to see self-centredness, self-indulgence, self-righteousness and self-pity. And I know there are more I've not yet discovered.

Selfishness is at the root of all human heartache. Instead of putting Christ on the throne of our hearts, we have placed SELF there. From infancy to old age, we love to have it 'our way'. And yet, when we get it 'our way', we are not happy and our hearts remain restless.

However, if we have received Christ's forgiveness and chosen to follow Him, God's Holy Spirit comes to live in us. His character is holy and pure and His desire is to work with us to change us into His likeness (2 Corinthians 3:18). This is the work of a lifetime. It is accomplished minute by minute, as each day we recognise our selfishness in a particular area and surrender it, allowing the nature of Jesus to take over. We are called to be honest with ourselves and honest before God. He knows anyway! This crucifying of 'self', although hard, is the only way to true freedom. Little by little, the 'old me' dies and the life of Jesus grows in me. As the apostle Paul wrote, 'I have been crucified with Christ and I no longer live, but Christ lives in me. The life I live in the body, I live by faith in the Son of God, who loved me and gave himself for me' (Galatians 2:20).

Just as in 'Pass the parcel' the prize was eventually revealed, so it will be for us if we choose to let Jesus be Lord in our lives. This is the pilgrim's progress. 'Thou has made for us Thyself, O Lord, and our hearts are restless until they rest in Thee' (*The Confessions of St Augustine*).

Dear Jesus, thank You for being my Saviour. Please help me to allow You to be Lord in my life. Thank You for the gift of the Holy Spirit to help me on my journey.

39. *The piano*

When I was fifteen we lived in a three-bedroomed council house with just two rooms downstairs. I had seven younger siblings at that time. Strangely, I didn't realise that we were overcrowded; one never thought of such things.

Almost seven decades later, as I reminisce about the piano, I'm utterly amazed. Let me tell you about it. We received a message one day from our Auntie Mary-Ellen. She told us that her neighbours were moving and if we'd like their piano we could have it. One would think that the reluctant reply should have been: 'Thank you, but we haven't got room for it.' But no, the answer was a fervent, 'Yes, please!'

I was filled with excitement as I awaited its arrival and it certainly made an entrance; it was a BIG piano. Made of walnut, with ivory and ebony keys, it had heavily carved legs and the front boasted a tapestry panel, two mirrors and two candle holders. Personally, I felt that we'd gone up in the world with this magnificent piece of furniture dominating our living room. My mother immediately taught us to play the one tune she'd learnt as a child. We loved it!

The next amazing happening was this. Before her marriage, my mother had worked as a housemaid for a family who had a friend called Percy. He was a blind piano tuner. She herself had a very good ear for music and could, quite naturally, sing a descant to any tune. She recognised that the piano was off-key so she decided that it would have to be tuned. I can't imagine

how they afforded it but Percy was contacted, and from then on he came regularly to tune our piano. He also persuaded my parents to let me have a few piano lessons. I was thrilled and my rapid progress delighted my teacher. My parents managed to let me have one year of lessons and, from there, I took off on my own. Family music-making was a joy. How our lives were changed because room was made for that piano! In later years I was able to bring music into the lives of many children in the schools where I taught. More wonderful for me still is that I have children and grandchildren whose musical gifts and their use of them are outstanding.

As I thought about this, I asked myself the question, 'What if we'd said that we didn't have room for the piano?' We'd never have known what we'd missed.

It's very much like that when Jesus knocks on the door of our hearts to ask whether we have room for Him. Many people say, 'No, I'm too busy; life is too full; there just isn't time or space!' Sadly, they'll never know what they've missed. But for those who say, 'Yes, I'll make room for You, Jesus,' life changes. The Holy Spirit gently tunes us in to the beat of Jesus' heart and, from then on, we sing a new song, harmonising with God's Song for our lives. And when we strike a wrong note, He corrects us, teaches us and leads us on.

The symphony of life has its moods and seasons but with Jesus in our hearts we will always be safe, secure in His promises, until we see Him face to face. Jesus says to each of us,

'Look! I have been standing at the door and I am constantly knocking. If you hear me calling you and open the door, I will come in and have fellowship with you and you with me' (adapted from Revelation 3:20, TLB).

Come, Lord Jesus, come. Maranatha.

When the time comes

How wonderful it is to know
One day I'll see Your face!
Those loving eyes will pierce my heart,
Those arms embrace.

And kneeling down before You,
I'll kiss those wounded feet.
My tears will flow with unknown love,
With unknown joy and peace.

Will You reach out and take my hand
In Your dear pierced one –
And lead me into blessedness
As one who is Your own?

Then glory will overwhelm me,
Radiance and angel song;
Father will haste to greet me,
As I enter with His Son.

Surprised by love and peace and joy,
I'll know at last I'm home
In the place You have prepared for me,
Prepared for that time to come.

Courses and seminars

Publishing and new media

Conference facilities

Transforming lives

CWR's vision is to enable people to experience personal transformation through applying God's Word to their lives and relationships.

Our Bible-based training and resources help people around the world to:
• Grow in their walk with God
• Understand and apply Scripture to their lives
• Resource themselves and their church
• Develop pastoral care and counselling skills
• Train for leadership
• Strengthen relationships, marriage and family life and much more.

CWR Applying God's Word
to everyday life and relationships

CWR, Waverley Abbey House,
Waverley Lane, Farnham,
Surrey GU9 8EP, UK

Telephone: +44 (0)1252 784700
Email: info@cwr.org.uk
Website: www.cwr.org.uk

Registered Charity No 294387
Company Registration No 1990308

Our insightful writers provide daily Bible-reading notes and other resources for all ages, and our experienced course designers and presenters have gained an international reputation for excellence and effectiveness.

CWR's Training and Conference Centre in Surrey, England, provides excellent facilities in an idyllic setting - ideal for both learning and spiritual refreshment.

National Distributors

UK: (and countries not listed below)
CWR, Waverley Abbey House, Waverley Lane, Farnham, Surrey GU9 8EP. Tel: (01252) 784700
Outside UK (44) 1252 784700 Email: mail@cwr.org.uk

AUSTRALIA: KI Entertainment, Unit 21 317-321 Woodpark Road, Smithfield, New South Wales 2164.
Tel: 1 800 850 777 Fax: 02 9604 3699 Email: sales@kientertainment.com.au

CANADA: David C Cook Distribution Canada, PO Box 98, 55 Woodslee Avenue, Paris, Ontario N3L 3E5.
Tel: 1800 263 2664 Email: sandi.swanson@davidccook.ca

GHANA: Challenge Enterprises of Ghana, PO Box 5723, Accra. Tel: (021) 222437/223249 Fax: (021) 226227
Email: ceg@africaonline.com.gh

HONG KONG: Cross Communications Ltd, 1/F, 562A Nathan Road, Kowloon. Tel: 2780 1188 Fax: 2770 6229
Email: cross@crosshk.com

INDIA: Crystal Communications, 10-3-18/4/1, East Marredpalli, Secunderabad – 500026, Andhra Pradesh.
Tel/Fax: (040) 27737145 Email: crystal_edwj@rediffmail.com

KENYA: Keswick Books and Gifts Ltd, PO Box 10242-00400, Nairobi. Tel: (020) 2226047/312639
Email: sales.keswick@africaonline.co.ke

MALAYSIA: Canaanland, No. 25 Jalan PJU 1A/41B, NZX Commercial Centre, Ara Jaya, 47301 Petaling Jaya, Selangor.
Tel: (03) 7885 0540/1/2 Fax: (03) 7885 0545 Email: info@canaanland.com.my

Salvation Publishing & Distribution Sdn Bhd, 23 Jalan SS 2/64, 47300 Petaling Jaya, Selangor.
Tel: (03) 78766411/78766797 Fax: (03) 78757066/78756360
Email: info@salvationbookcentre.com

NEW ZEALAND: KI Entertainment, Unit 21 317-321 Woodpark Road, Smithfield, New South Wales 2164, Australia.
Tel: 0 800 850 777 Fax: +612 9604 3699 Email: sales@kientertainment.com.au

NIGERIA: FBFM, Helen Baugh House, 96 St Finbarr's College Road, Akoka, Lagos.
Tel: (01) 7747429/4700218/825775/827264 Email: fbfm_1@yahoo.com

PHILIPPINES: OMF Literature Inc, 776 Boni Avenue, Mandaluyong City. Tel: (02) 531 2183 Fax: (02) 531 1960
Email: gloadlaon@omflit.com

SINGAPORE: Alby Commercial Enterprises Pte Ltd, 95 Kallang Avenue #04-00, AIS Industrial Building, 339420.
Tel: (65) 629 27238 Fax: (65) 629 27235 Email: marketing@alby.com.sg

SOUTH AFRICA: Struik Christian Books, 80 MacKenzie Street, PO Box 1144, Cape Town 8000. Tel: (021) 462 4360
Fax: (021) 461 3612 Email: info@struikchristianmedia.co.za

SRI LANKA: Christombu Publications (Pvt) Ltd, Bartleet House, 65 Braybrooke Place, Colombo 2.
Tel: (9411) 2421073/2447665 Email: dhanad@bartleet.com

USA: David C Cook Distribution Canada, PO Box 98, 55 Woodslee Avenue, Paris, Ontario N3L 3E5, Canada.
Tel: 1800 263 2664 Email: sandi.swanson@davidccook.ca

CWR is a Registered Charity – Number 294387
CWR is a Limited Company registered in England – Registration Number 1990308

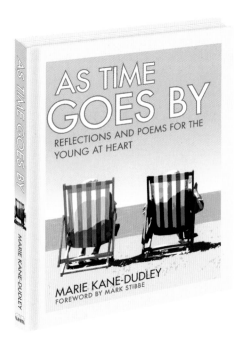

Learn profound truths from simple stories

This charming book contains 52 more modern-day parables, personal stories and reflections written by Marie Kane-Dudley. It will take you into the heart of someone very special who has lived through times of great change.

Short, simple prayers will move you closer to the God who loves us faithfully as time goes by.

As Time Goes By
by Marie Kane-Dudley
148-page hardback, full-colour, 147x187mm
ISBN: 978-1-85345-487-5

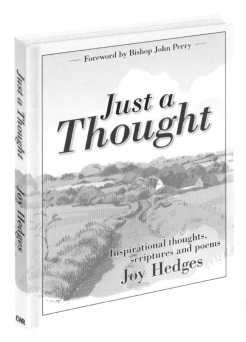

A collection of inspirational thoughts, scriptures and poems

Through fifty inspirational articles and eight poems, newspaper columnist Joy Hedges shares how God has touched her life through art, nature and friendship, providing a glimpse of the power of God working in everyday life. Full colour throughout and featuring beautiful watercolours, this item makes an ideal gift!

Just a Thought
by Joy Hedges
128-page hardback, full-colour, 147x187mm
ISBN: 978-1-85345-600-8

To order or for more information, including current prices,
visit **www.cwr.org.uk/store** or a Christian bookshop.

Daily devotionals

Our range of daily Bible-reading notes has something for everyone – and to engage with even the most demanding members of the family!

Whether you want themed devotional writing, life-application notes, a deeper Bible study or meditations tailored to women or the growing minds of children and young people, we have just the one for you.

To order or for more information, including current prices, visit **www.cwr.org.uk/store** or a Christian bookshop.